T0171607

Bliss
every day

a practical guide to
find peace and happiness

Deborah Fairfull

iUniverse, Inc.
Bloomington

Bliss every day
a practical guide to find peace and happiness

iUniverse books may be ordered through booksellers or by contacting:

*iUniverse
1663 Liberty Drive
Bloomington, IN 47403
www.iuniverse.com
1-800-Authors (1-800-288-4677)*

*Because of the dynamic nature of the Internet, any web addresses or links
contained in this book may have changed since publication and may no
longer be valid.*

ISBN: 978-1-4502-2985-2 (sc)
ISBN: 978-1-4502-2984-5 (ebk)

Printed in the United States of America

iUniverse rev. date: 5/9/2011

For three shining lights:
Sierra, Ewan, and Scarlett

Someone once said to Mahatma Gandhi:

"Mahatmaji, you are an exceptional man. You must not expect the world to act as you do."

Gandhi replied:

"It is curious how we delude ourselves, fancying that the body can be improved, but that it is impossible to evoke the hidden powers of the soul. I am engaged in trying to show if I have any of those powers, I am as frail a mortal as any of us and that I never had anything extraordinary about me nor have I now. I am a simple individual liable to err like any other fellow mortal. I own, however, that I have enough humility to confess my errors and to retrace my steps. I own that I have immovable faith in God and his goodness, and an unconsumable passion for truth and love. But is that not what every person has latent in him?"

Contents

preface

my first daughter, Sierra, was born at 2:11AM on October 7, 1997. She was completely alert and had the most enormous eyes. She didn't cry at all; she was perfectly peaceful. Her eyes looked deep into mine as if to say, "Hello, so you're my mummy. That's what you look like! I now have an image to match the voice I've been hearing for the past nine months."

Later a nurse took Sierra and put her in a cot near the bed. She immediately began to cry. The nurse said, "She wants to be with you." She placed her next to me, and we snuggled up and fell asleep until morning—pure bliss.

I believe Sierra paved the way for my spiritual awakening.

About eighteen months later I attended a metaphysical mastery seminar to learn about Deepak Chopra's approach to well-being. I was planning to open a healthy fast-food restaurant and thought some of the ideas could be helpful. I didn't know anything about metaphysics at the time; however, other speakers that day included Louise Hay, Wayne Dyer, James Redfield, Michael Rowland, Terra Collins, and Leon Nacson.

It was a day that touched my soul.

Each spoke of spiritual principles based on his or her perceptions and experiences. After the seminar had finished, later that evening, I spontaneously found myself in a state of pure joy and bliss. The yogis refer to this experience as *ananda*. They are referring to a return back to an underlying depth that is within every individual. It is an experience of enjoyment, beneath the differences of personality. I felt in perfect flow with life. I felt the perfection and beauty within myself and witnessed it in everyone around me. I had unlimited energy and felt infinitely happy. For the first time in my life, I had a deep knowing of how the universe worked. *Everything made perfect sense!* I had the *experience* that everything else and I was pure love.

This state of love and joy lasted for three days—I thought it would never end—until I came out of it with a thud. I was back to where I was before. It was not that my life was bad or difficult. It was just that the pure ease, joy, and flow had gone, and I returned to the *normal* experience of life. I was later to understand I had experienced a spiritual awakening.

During the seminar Wayne Dyer spoke of principles of manifestation using the *japa* meditation he'd learned in India. I practiced this meditation daily without expectation. During this time my husband and I together were able to manifest results beyond our wildest dreams, in terms of material success.

Wayne Dyer had asked during the seminar if anyone would like to come to Peru with him and his family. I knew I would be there. The trip was for forty days, roaming the ancient sites of the Aztecs, including the spectacular mountains of Machu Picchu. On the mountaintops I felt like I could almost touch the sun. On our last evening we celebrated our time together at a beautiful floating restaurant on the waters of Lima. It was a magic night. The entire group sang the Barney song *I love you, you love me* to Sierra, who was then two years old.

Later that evening, as I lay in bed looking out over the sprawling city lights of Lima, I felt completely merged with everything, and everything was merged with me. It was a feeling of total oneness of intense joy and bliss. That extremely peaceful feeling remained for nine months. This was a more intense experience than my awakening. During the first experience, I could feel the total love and perfection in everything. In the second experience, I felt at one with everything in existence.

When I arrived back in Australia, I began a new start-up business called Eatsmart that sold healthy fast-food. The set-up flowed effortlessly and joyfully, even though it was an intensely busy time. Eatsmart opened its doors, and for the first eighteen months I found running the business extremely challenging. After this difficult establishment phase, the business turned the corner and became profitable, and I felt the financial pressure ease. About a year later I was fortunate enough to be blessed with my beautiful baby boy, Ewan.

When Ewan was about a year old, I remember a particularly memorable moment: I was standing in the lounge room of my beautiful home at Chinaman's Beach at dusk. I felt very happy and peaceful. My ninety-one-year-old grandmother was staying with me. We went to sit on the beach to watch the twilight sailing. The boats drifting back into the harbour was an incredibly beautiful sight. In that moment I felt I had everything. A special connection with my grandmother, a wonderful husband, two beautiful children, and a gorgeous home in the most idyllic location I could imagine. This was all right in the heart of one of the most beautiful cities in the world. We also had many investment properties and Eatsmart was now winning awards. *I had no idea of what was to come!*

About a year later my life started to change dramatically. I sold Eatsmart, knowing that it was only part of my journey. Although I loved the business and what it offered the community, I was looking to do work that was my true purpose. I did not know exactly where my journey was taking me—only that working in the area of human development was a passion and integral to my path.

I also wanted to develop a lifestyle where I could spend more time with my family. In the month that followed the sale of the business I was overjoyed to discover that I was going to have my third baby. Toward the end of that year, my angelic daughter Scarlett arrived.

Around this time my financial situation began to decline. My husband and I lost most of what we had and we sold our properties. All of this put an incredible strain on our relationship and we separated. Depression set in. How could I go from having *everything* to having so much less, in a material sense?

I wanted to know why this was so. The next four years were to be some of the most difficult of my entire life. I began a journey of self-discovery. I shifted focus to my internal world. Although

I was experiencing a difficult period, I hadn't forgotten the states of bliss I had previously experienced. If this state was possible before, I felt innately it must be possible to experience again. I wanted to know: "Is it possible to feel peaceful and happy on a permanent basis*?" I had so many unanswered questions.*

Using myself as a case study, I examined things such as, "What creates sustainable joy and happiness?" "What things take us away from these states, and how are we able to bring ourselves back to our peace?" "How do we find our true purpose in life?".

I sensed that finding the answers to these questions was one of the most important things I could do. I was on a path, consciously working out, step by step, how to create the states of bliss, peace, and joy that matched the feelings I had experienced before. I felt that if I, an *ordinary* person—as opposed to a guru or yogi—was able to experience deep inner peace, perfection, and oneness spontaneously, wouldn't it then be possible for anybody? I also wanted to learn how to feel like this on a more permanent basis.

During this time I studied kinesiology, counselling, and psychotherapy. I incorporated yogic principles and philosophy. I looked deeply into the connection between mind, body, and spirit by studying my unconscious, behavioural patterns, thoughts, and beliefs.

I came to understand the philosophy of impermanence. Businesses, wealth, and people can come and go in life. I discovered the true source of self-esteem comes from having a deep and loving relationship with your life. It is like building your world on a solid foundation.

External success can mask how a person really feels inside. But once you have tapped into your true internal sense of self-worth, it is permanent and real. It's not something anything or anyone else can ever take away.

From this strong and solid place there are no limits to what can be achieved in terms of relationships, success, and material abundance. True empowerment comes from love rather than fear. Living your life from a loving perspective is the most important gift you can give yourself and everyone around you.

Judgment maintains the division and fear that many people experience. *The more we are in our head, we judge, the more we are in our heart, we love.* If we are holding onto past hurts, it can be difficult to feel and express love. Hurt is healed by understanding and forgiveness. I found once I was able to forgive and accept others and myself lovingly, when tension arose, I was more readily able to remain connected to my internal loving state. When I loved myself regardless of my faults, ego, or *shadow side* (a psychological term to describe the unconscious or unknown parts of ourselves), I could then be more loving and benevolent. From this loving, accepting place, I could develop new skills to change my behaviour if I wanted to. I found the most natural way to return to my loving state was by accepting responsibility for my reactions, forgiving others and myself, being present, and learning new skills in areas where I was struggling. Underlying this was the principle of being authentic—being true to myself and living life guided by my intuition.

I then set up a kinesiology practice incorporating many of the things I had learned on my own journey. Through my work I witnessed clients experiencing shifts and changes that brought them closer to their natural state of peace and happiness.

This is a time in history when many people are facing challenging times. What they thought provided security is no longer there for them. They are wondering where to turn. Every crisis offers the world a chance to turn loss into opportunity. *Is a crisis the end, or is it just the beginning?*

This is our opportunity to evolve to a world based on hope joy, and love—rather than fear, hatred, and division. This evolution is not going to occur by changing the world, but by changing our perspective of life to one of love.

Joy is not things, it is in us.
~ Richard Wagner

acknowledgments

o Mum and Dad, for your ongoing love and support and just for being yourselves. To my three children: Sierra, Ewan and Scarlett. Thank you for your sense of humour and the gift of sharing the way you look at the world. Thanks to David, for your kindness and gentle strength.

Thanks to Nana, for your sparkling joy and dynamic approach towards life. To my other grandmother whose peaceful presence and calm centeredness was joyful to be around. Thanks to both my grandfathers for your integrity and unconditional love. To my brother Gary and sister Tanya, for all the fun along the way.

To my large and extended family, with whom I am fortunate to share many carefree and blissful times. Thanks to Aunty Lorraine for your passion for life and to Aunty Elaine for being a second mum.

To Ron Symes, for your fantastic talent in developing the illustrations and dedication to getting them just right. Thank you to Elise Lockwood for your beautiful spirit and photography. To Helene Drimer for your loving care and attention to detail in fine-tuning the book. To dearest Basia for your help with proofreading. To Anne for your creative ideas and valuable feedback.

To Natalie and Irma, for your gorgeousness and beautiful kinesiology balances. To my incredible kinesiology colleagues: Irma (again), Ellie, Kim, Nathan, Jo, Anne, Helen, Suzie, Cyrus, Emma, and Debbie.

For my friends with huge hearts and loving wisdom: Fiona, Anne-Marie, Deborah, Liana, Sally, Suzanne, Rebecca, Lisa, Chloe, Victoria, Tracey, Cathy, Joanne, Barbara, Leslie, Kate, Elise, Jenny, Anne, and Sofia.

To the fabulous and inspiring practitioners that I have worked with: Helene, Shalom, Sarah, Rebecca, Ali, Glenda, and Prue. Thanks to my teachers Nick, David, Matt, Robert, Duncan, and Keenan.

To Jesus and Paramahansa Yogananda, for your inspiration and gentle presence.

introduction

You are love, pure love—that is your essence. Love is who you truly are—only some of you have forgotten. This book is a call to remember who you are, love. There is not one exception. Pure divine love, all the rest is not real—only defences and protection that have built up over the years. These are the layers that you *think* you need to keep you safe. *Think* is a very important word here, as it means you are in your head. But it is in your heart space that joy, happiness, love, and contentment reside.

It is possible to think that you need to judge and analyse others to keep you safe and know what is right for you, but this ultimately creates division. If you let go of judgment and approach others with an open heart, your intuition will guide you on your path to happiness.

It is the ego that convinces you that suffering, division, and constantly needing more are all part of life. This is not true.

Collectively we can rise above this way of thinking and create an even more beautiful world of peace, love, and harmony.

You are designed to be a full expression of your loving self. Experiences in your life that hurt can be used to create a harder *shell* as a defense. Alternatively, you can use your everyday, direct experiences—even the challenging ones—to evolve and develop greater understanding and become more open and loving.

The challenges of life can be used as alchemy for love. Shining light on our experiences, even painful ones, can turn our relationships with ourself and other people into a great source of joy.

<hr>

how to use the
practical support section

The practical ideas sections of this book are to give useful tools to help you feel peaceful and happy. It is not necessary to do all of them but instead the ones you resonate with, in the areas of your life, you would like to master.

Different approaches or techniques will work for you in various situations. The practical support section is designed to be a smorgasbord of ideas for you to choose from.

chapter one

tune into
your body

your body is the most amazing super computer you will ever find. It constantly gives you feedback to maintain your well-being and happiness. When you begin to tune into what your body is telling you, it allows you to be proactive in relation to your health. However, if you ignore the signals of your body, it can create disconnection between your mind and body. Over time, if this continues, things such as emotional instability or disease could develop.

Pain is designed to give you messages about yourself. When you are unwell it can be helpful to make the connection between what is happening in your body and what is going on in your mind and external world. For example, if you have *repeated* headaches, they are the body's warning sign that something needs attention. The headaches could be occurring regularly at work. It would then make sense to investigate if they are related to work. Changes may need to be made to improve work in some way. You may need to talk to someone, change your career or, change your thinking or perception in relation to work. When you know what you need to do and appropriate changes are made, your headaches will usually disappear.

Unfortunately, the body's signals are often ignored when they are small. When signals and symptoms are minor, adjustments to get the body back into balance are much easier to make.

Dr Bruce Lipton is a leading-edge biologist. His research shows that it is not genes and DNA that control our biology, but instead it is signals from outside our cells. These signals include the energetic messages that come from positive and negative thoughts. Your beliefs and thoughts can have a major influence on your health.

To begin to tune into how your body and thoughts (mind) work together in relation to your well-being, it is helpful to be aware of the three stages of stress:

1. **Stage 1:** Signals at this stage place a slight, *short-term* stress on the body that passes quickly. For example, if you lose your keys, you might feel anxious when looking for them. However, the anxiety passes once the keys are found. Awareness comes by asking, "Why am I repeatedly losing my keys?" The answer could

be that you are doing too much or need a regular spot to put them. If notice is taken when the signals are in Stage 1, adjustments are relatively easy to make.

It is also useful to be aware of what you are thinking while you are trying to find the keys. Thoughts such as, "I'm late, I'll never get there. I can't believe I've lost the keys again," usually make matters worse. However, if you are mindful of your thoughts and think, "I'm sure they'll turn up" or "What was I doing when I last had them?" you are more likely to find them quickly. Your thought processes are supporting you. Your mind and body are working together.

Another option is to try to relax for a moment to calm your mind. When you are relaxed it is easier for your memory and intuition to function, which will help to guide you to the place you last left your keys. That is why you will often remember something when you stop trying to think about it. Have you ever found that when you stop trying to force the answer to your problem, the solution will just come to you, for example when you are in the shower?

2. **Stage 2:** This next stage generally occurs when Stage 1 signals are not listened to. Stage 2 stress manifests physically in the body. This is the body's way of stepping up the pressure for you to look at what is going on in your life. Stage 2 stress manifests in illness, such as the flu, irritable bowel syndrome, migraines, depression, and panic attacks. It is often at this stage that the help of a professional, such as a therapist or doctor, is sought.

When someone identifies the link between the illness and what is causing the illness, it can aid the healing process. For example, if you are constantly losing the keys and ignore why, over a period of time you could also develop panic attacks. You might then be motivated to find out why you are having the panic attacks. It could be because you feel overloaded with work and cannot see a way to resolve the issue. If you take responsibility and look at why you are taking on so much work and develop awareness around the thought processes and attitudes that are driving you, it is possible to make positive, lasting changes.

Consistent thoughts manifest as beliefs, and consistently held beliefs become attitudes that determine behaviour. Your attitudes steer your life, like a rudder determines the course of a boat. Attitudes are held in the body's physical structures and in the biochemistry of the body as energetic patterns. (Krebs, 2001, 102). Positive attitudes affect the body in a positive way, making you feel lighter and more energetic. Negative attitudes that remain unchanged, over a period of time can form as disease in the body. Attitudes are often unconscious, and illness can be an opportunity to increase self-awareness and change to positive attitudes that support health and well-being.

3.   **Stage 3:** If Stage 2 stress is not healed at a deep level, a more serious illness may develop to urge someone to take notice of the imbalances in their life. For example, it is possible to ignore *why* the panic attacks are reoccurring and choose to medicate instead. If this happens for a prolonged period, a Stage 3 illness could develop. This is because medicating while repeating the same thoughts and behaviours is not treating the root cause of the illness and it is more likely to return. Stage 3 illnesses are usually serious and more difficult to resolve, for example, cancer, arthritis, heart problems, and gall stones. It is possible to heal Stage 3 illnesses; however, it is more difficult than dealing with an issue at Stage 1.

Your body wants you to be well and happy. It will give you signals to tell you when you are out of balance. It is important to listen and determine the real meaning of what your body is saying.

You can take a Band-Aid or quick-fix approach by overriding the messages to avoid worrying about it now. Alternatively, you could take the time to find out what is really going on and make the necessary adjustments. By linking what is physically happening in your body to your thoughts, you can begin to return to your natural state of wellness.

If you are already ill, it may be an opportunity to teach you more about yourself. Illness is not a weakness or a call to judge yourself or others in any way. Your ego (see chapter 13) would have you believe that being ill is your fault, and nothing could be further from the truth. Illness for some is a step on the path of their journey to love. If you are ill, it can give you an opportunity to expand your awareness in some way.

When I was in my late twenties, I had glandular fever. I was working incredibly long hours in my first business and was not supporting myself enough nutritionally for my lifestyle. This illness gave me the opportunity to study nutrition and educated me in a way that I have adopted positive lifelong eating habits. I also made lifestyle changes in terms of less work and more recreation. I needed to create more balance in my life. I had many signals along the way but ignored them until I was seriously ill and bedridden, giving me time to think about my choices!

When your body is run down stressed and exhausted, I have found that it can be helpful to get professional structural and biochemical support. Chiropractors, osteopaths, naturopaths and nutritionalists can be very effective in giving your body support to help it function at its optimum.

Lovingly listen to your body and take action in relation to what it is telling you in order to create well-being and happiness.

Your body wants you to be well and happy.

practical support

Develop an overall knowledge of physical body systems and what they relate to emotionally. The table below is a brief overview:

Table 1: Relating mind and body

Physical disease	Emotions	Key to balance
Stomach/Spleen Digestion issues, blood sugar regulation, irregular breathing	Over-thinking, worry, obsession	Aligning with your true purpose.
Heart/Small Intestines Anxiety, stress, sleeping issues, emotional imbalance, skin problems, blood pressure, memory issues	Lack of joy, sadness, feeling disconnected	Clarity to be in tune with the flow of life. Knowing what is right for you.
Lungs/Colon Respiratory issues, sinus, allergies, issues with elimination of waste	Grief, sadness, guilt	Connecting to and valuing your spirit.
Kidneys/Bladder Urination issues, water retention, backache, joint pain or swelling, bone issues	Fear, control, indecision, timidness	Following your intuition. Using your will to create the life you desire.
Liver/Gallbladder Arthritis, migraine, headaches, dizziness, vision issues, fatigue	Defensiveness, anger, frustration, irritability	Accepting yourself as you grow toward empowerment.

chapter two

make peace
with your past

making peace with your past helps you to experience the present more fully. In a present state your attitude toward life becomes lighter. If thoughts about the past are negative, they can consume your energy and make you feel heavy and tired. If you are carrying resentment or unresolved issues from the past (often these are unconscious), it can be difficult to feel truly happy. You may find you are not fully in the "here and now" and able to absorb the true beauty of life, which occurs moment to moment.

Unresolved issues from the past can often result in *seeing problems in others that don't really belong to them*. The problems can be a reflection of how you are really feeling inside. In the world of psychology, this is called *projection*. Projection can be a wonderful tool to learn more about you. If you see problems in others, it can be helpful to take responsibility for how you feel rather than blaming them. This gives you the opportunity to learn more about what your feelings are trying to tell you. When others have certain feelings that gives them the opportunity to learn more about themselves. When people take responsibility for other people's feelings, this is called *codependency*. It is wise to take responsibility for your feelings and let other people take responsibility for theirs; this gives everyone a sense of empowerment and freedom.

The first step toward letting go of any unresolved feelings is to accept them. For example, before someone can learn to process anger constructively, they have to accept and take responsibility that they have a problem dealing with anger. From this place of acceptance, rather than denial, you can move to where you would like to be. Change begins with awareness. You maintain the things you resist. All pain is resistance of some sort.

When left unresolved, uncomfortable or unhappy feelings about the past can weigh you down physically and emotionally. This is often referred to as *baggage*. Baggage can spill over to others and create unpleasant relationships.

Insight regarding yourself and expanding your awareness are the keys to creating a peaceful relationship within yourself and with the people around you. The quality of your current relationships is usually a good indicator of the peace you feel within.

For example, you may continually find yourself in relationships where your partner leaves you and you feel abandoned. You may begin to feel frustrated and annoyed that this situation keeps *reoccurring* in your life. You could keep blaming your partners *or* take responsibility by looking at your own patterns to see why the same situation keeps happening.

When you take responsibility for your patterns you begin to develop the skills to create your life from choice. Upon further investigation, you may realise that when you were five years old your father suddenly left the family and you felt abandoned. You did not fully express and process your emotions around your father leaving at the time. The feelings from this situation keep coming to the surface in your current relationships, giving you the opportunity to heal them. These feelings will generally reoccur until you consciously understand why the feelings are there in the first place. This will help you grow and develop emotionally. Rather than continually recreating the same patterns in your life, you will be able to consciously create the relationship you desire.

When you confront, accept, and integrate unresolved issues, you will find the quality of your day-to-day life improves. The energy used to hold down, or *repress*, unhappy memories will instead be used to create a more joyous life.

You are designed for well-being and happiness. Your body keeps giving you signals to guide you toward this natural state.

If life is viewed as a teacher, it then becomes just that. Unless the painful lessons of life, which we deal ourselves, are transformed, through humility, into gateways to growth and development, they are wasted (Hawkins, 1995, 204).

You may find yourself in unwanted situations, until you learn the lesson. For example, you might find yourself feeling overlooked at work. You may leave and continue to find yourself feeling overlooked at the next place you work. When you stop blaming the external situation—work—and see it as a reoccurring pattern within you, you will be able to make some lasting changes. By confronting the feeling of being overlooked, which you may have felt at various stages throughout your life, you will be getting to the core of the issue. You may have come from a large family and constantly felt overlooked, for example. The patterns we have inside us are reflected in our outer world. *As it is within, so it is without.*

Becoming consciously aware of the pattern and even voicing it out loud can sometimes be enough to heal it. This is because when you are conscious of a situation, you are able to make choices around it. If you are unconscious regarding your behaviour or patterns, they make the choices and drive you. That is how you end up in situations you don't want, as though you are on autopilot!

If you have been involved in a trauma in the past and did not have the opportunity to move through the natural stages of healing, such as anger, sadness, hurt, and peace—it can be beneficial to look at the issue. For example, if you suffered some sort of abuse while you were young, you may have problems trusting people as an adult. However, it can be helpful to come to a place of peace and compassion regarding any former abusive incidents, letting them go and recognising they had nothing to do with you. This helps you to form more loving relationships as an adult.

A neutral sounding board can be very effective in helping to release any unresolved feelings around traumas and understand your unconscious and/or your behavioural patterns. Working with a therapist can be helpful during this phase. A good therapist sees you as the divine, loving individual you are and facilitates your discovery of solutions, from your own wisdom. Just by hearing yourself speak in an environment of unconditional love can allow you to gain clarity and insights.

Holding onto hurts and issues past or present will often manifest as resentment in you. For your well-being, no matter how difficult it may seem, it is very healing to let go of resentment toward any other person in your life, no matter how badly they hurt you. *Holding onto resentment ultimately only hurts you.* When you let go of resentment and hurt, you are able to be in tune with the love that inherently lives within you. This process may take time, but is ultimately worth it on the journey towards peace of mind. See the forgiveness exercise at the end of the chapter for practical support.

Acceptance and forgiveness are powerful tools in achieving inner peace. Insight and understanding will help you see that everybody does the best they can with the skills they have at the time, and this applies to you too! I believe there are no exceptions to this rule. Seeing and understanding are the way to love and compassion. When we view our own and others' *humanness* with kindness, then the world will evolve to being more peaceful and harmonious. The journey begins with us!

Everyone has a past. The difference is whether you let your past unconsciously drive you to act out behaviours that you later regret or to be involved in situations that make you unhappy. Unhealthy relationships, drinking problems, gambling, smoking, overworking and/or overeating are examples of behaviours people engage in to stop feeling painful feelings. This ultimately only *numbs* the feelings and prolongs the healing process. If addictions have formed in the areas of alcohol, drugs, and/or gambling, for example, professional groups such as Alcoholics Anonymous may be required. Such groups provide loving support and are experts in teaching people in how to deal with their feelings in ways other than addiction and its harmful side effects.

Once you begin to understand your past and how it affects your behaviours, you can live your life with greater awareness. You will no longer try to escape from yourself or the feelings that you don't understand and have kept buried because they don't feel good. Once you validate how you really feel about things, you remove the *emotional charge,* or the energy, around certain situations. When you have an emotional charge around something, you have strong positive or negative feelings that can drive your behaviour.

When you lovingly accept yourself and others as neither good nor bad, it makes life easier to accept as it is. This allows you to flow with life rather than fight against it. Resistance to "what is" requires energy that could be used to enjoy present experiences.

When you accept your past as it was, you can begin to understand the way it has helped shape your character giving you unique qualities, insights, and depth that you may not have otherwise experienced. Your life's journey can be a wonderful teacher, helping you to develop compassion, expand your awareness, and open your heart.

As it is within, so it is without.

practical support

This exercise is helpful to feel at peace with someone in your life—past or present. Use a separate piece of paper and write it down in your own handwriting. When you have finished throw away or burn the exercise, to symbolize letting go of any unresolved feelings.

I let go of my resentment/hurt/fear/judgment towards

_____.

I move on and create a *new loving* chapter in my life.
I release any unresolved feelings I have toward_____
and realize that he or she is doing the best he or she can with the skills he or she has, just as I am.

We are all perfect as we are.

I release any judgements/expectations of others and myself and choose to deeply love myself and to flow with life.

I love _____ and choose to *let him or her and myself free.*

chapter three

feel your feelings

o experience and express love, you need to be able to feel. *Love is a feeling.* Joy, peace, happiness, and contentment are all feelings. To experience feelings you need to allow them to flow through your body.

When you are in touch with and are able to express your feelings, it allows you to be authentic and congruent. *Authentic* means being real and genuine. *Congruent* means saying what you feel in the present moment, as opposed to feeling something and saying something else. When you are genuine, people sense it and you are more likely to connect with them on a deep and meaningful level. The exception is if you have a reaction and speak based on the resulting feelings. Speaking as a result of a reaction can create confusion and blame. Telling someone your feelings in the *heat of the moment* without processing your reaction first, does not usually lead to closeness and connection (see chapter 5 for how to deal with reactions).

The most common way to resist feeling is to keep busy going from one thing to the next, without a break, or time to just be. It is easier to become aware of your feelings when it is still and quiet. If there are any unresolved feelings of hurt from the past, staying busy can be a way to prevent these feelings from surfacing. However, these feelings drive your body anyway, in terms of unconscious patterns and behaviours. To be in tune with your feelings you need time and space to feel them—rather than drowning them out with *busyness*. If unresolved painful feelings come to the surface, it is beneficial to recognise and observe them, rather than having them drive you in a way you may not desire.

When you resist how you really feel, tension is created within your body that stops you from flowing energetically. You can even mistakenly identify yourself as the feeling rather than observing the feeling. For example, you may think you are a sad person rather than just having a sad moment, which if you acknowledge and don't resist, will pass in time.

If you continue to ignore your feelings they can build up as emotional pain, and this can in turn manifest as physical pain in your body. *All pain is caused by resistance to what is.* Pain in itself is not a bad thing; it is there to give you information about yourself. Listen to your pain when it is small, if possible. It may be telling you to take action, make changes, or let go in certain areas of your life.

It is easy to ignore true feelings, wanting to be happy all the time. However, this can create an internal struggle as natural emotions are resisted. You can be a happy person yet experience a sad moment. It is better for your health to observe the feeling and let it flow through your body rather than resist it or push it away (known as repression). Generally, once you allow your feeling to flow, you will then return to your natural state of happiness. The amount of time this takes depends on the situation.

Once my mother stayed with us for an extended period. When she was leaving, my four-year-old daughter and I waved her off as she drove away in the car. We then sat down on the front step and had a good cry because we were both sad she was leaving. There was a certain beauty in being really present to how we felt and expressing it in the moment.

It is common to search for a quick fix or instant gratification in relation to happiness—by shopping, taking drugs, drinking alcohol, working, or consuming food. *Excess* in any of these areas ultimately creates an imbalance and leaves you feeling dissatisfied. Imbalance shows that something needs to be addressed to allow you to return to a natural state of well-being. Instant gratification is like a Band-Aid approach to life, rather than being deeply in touch with what makes you truly happy.

The problem arises when you override your true feelings with messages from your head. If this is done over long periods of time, it can result in alienation or disconnection from how you really feel. For example, your body may be feeling tired, telling you to rest, and yet you ignore it, pushing yourself to a point of exhaustion or even illness. It is ideal to be in tune with how you really feel, and then you can take the appropriate action to take care of yourself.

Small children are generally in touch with the full range of feelings. They naturally let feelings flow freely through their bodies. If you observe them, they can be sad one minute, happy the next, angry ten minutes later, and then happy again. They do this without any guilt or resistance: that is, until they are taught to judge their feelings as *good* or *bad*. Accepting a child's feelings and teaching them to express them in healthy ways, helps them to feel acknowledged and valued.

As a child you may have been taught that only certain feelings were acceptable and others, such as anger and sadness, were not. As an adult, you may find it difficult to tune in with and express your feelings, in a way that can be heard and respected. *Fortunately these skills can be regained.*

First, you need to *observe* and *validate* how you are feeling. Resisting how you feel leads to repression, which is not healthy for your mind or body. If feelings are repressed rather than expressed in a healthy way, they weigh you down energetically. They make you feel heavy and disconnected from your natural state of wellness.

When you acknowledge your feelings, no matter what they are, you are able to live your life in a more congruent and authentic way. *You then have a choice*—to observe and let the feeling go *or* to respond to what that feeling is telling you. It is a sign of emotional maturity to be able to experience even the most uncomfortable feelings without acting out or reacting to someone else in a way that will hurt them. It is important to learn to sit with the discomfort that some feelings produce, until clarity about the appropriate action arrives. Maybe no overt action is necessary. Sometimes feelings arise to teach you something more about *yourself* (more about this in chapter 5 about reactions).

It is a gift to the people in your life to be able to sit with the discomfort of their feelings, without reacting to them. The exception is, if a person expresses their feelings in a violent or dangerous way, creating an unsafe environment for you. They would need to know that this is *not okay for you* and that they need to take responsibility for their own feelings. It can be helpful to seek the support of a professional if the feelings are very intense and overwhelming. Generally, it is very beneficial to allow people to have their feelings without judgement or taking things personally. This gives them the opportunity to explore and learn more about *themselves.*

You are not the feeling. A feeling is just a feeling. Observing a feeling without reacting is an important life-skill in terms of creating emotional stability. You may feel bad during a particular moment, but that does not make you a *bad* person. It is okay to feel annoyed with people from time to time, if that is how you really feel. It is important to validate all your feelings. *How you behave in relation to the feeling is the important thing.* You have a *choice* in relation to what you do with your feelings. Do you react to the feeling and perhaps yell at a person who annoyed you, or do you respond in an emotionally mature way? Are you able to sit with that uncomfortable feeling of annoyance until you work out what you need to do? The feeling may be a reaction you need to work through (see chapter 5), or it may be appropriate to share how you are feeling with another person *when you can do so in a loving way* (see chapter 10 for communicating with others).

Acknowledging your feelings as they are opens you up to understanding and knowing yourself and others at a deeper level. When you are able to feel your feelings, rather than a *fast-food* approach, you learn a deeply satisfying, sustainable approach to happiness that nourishes you like a nutritious meal.

It is important not to impulsively act on feelings but instead learn to observe them without judgement. Feelings let you tune into yourself and give you valuable information to guide you on your path to well-being and happiness.

All pain is caused by resistance to what is.

practical support

- Allow space in your life to feel. When you are quiet your feelings are more likely to surface. To do this:
  - Create time to sit quietly somewhere, for example, at the park or at home in your favourite chair.
  - Observe any feelings that arise, without judgement or analysis.
  - Let your feelings flow through your body without reacting to them.
  - Developing this skill will help you to respond rather than react to situations in your external world.
- Practice validating your own and others' feelings without judgement. This will help you to feel valued and to value others unique perception of life, even though its different from yours.

chapter four

make your
mind your friend

your mind is your most powerful tool in creating the life you want. When stressed or overwhelmed by circumstances, retraining your mind can allow you to remain peaceful, regardless of what is going on around you.

Most people do not *consciously* want a difficult life full of hardship and struggle. This type of life is created *unconsciously*. Observing the thoughts of your mind allows you to go beyond judgement and begin to live life from a state of awareness and peace. This is the difference between living an unconscious or a conscious life—the difference between being awake or asleep!

The Dalai Lama, the Tibetan head of state and spiritual leader, is a good example of someone who has a peaceful mind, regardless of external challenges. The Chinese are ruling his people against their will. The Dalai Lama is able to reach more people with his message of love and compassion—while his mind is calm and centred. This way of being is not only available to the Dalai Lama; it is available to anyone who desires to retrain his or her mind to be peaceful.

As you become comfortable with your feelings rather than overwhelmed by them (chapter 3), you will increase your capacity to be aware of your thoughts. *In fact, thoughts and feelings are the same.* A feeling occurs as a result of a thought—generally repeated thoughts. If you think repeatedly, "I love my life, I love my life," it is likely to be accompanied by a warm feeling of happiness in your body. Alternatively, if you *repeatedly* think, "I hate my life, I hate my life," you will probably feel sad, if not depressed.

Feelings and thoughts can fluctuate on a daily basis, depending on the external environment. However, if you learn to be in touch with your feelings and aware of your thoughts, you can learn to master your internal state—in many cases, *regardless of external forces*. When you are aware or able to develop the ability to observe your thoughts and feelings rather than becoming overwhelmed or driven by them, you will begin to live life in a conscious way. Obviously, in extreme cases of survival, lack of food, clothing, and/or shelter, this can be very difficult. The story of Victor Frankl is an amazing example of mental resilience in extreme circumstances.

Victor Frankl was able to master his internal state no matter what was going on around him. He was kept prisoner for three years in World War II concentration camps, where his parents and other close family members died. Victor survived by holding onto the love and image of his wife. The thought he held onto in almost unbearable conditions was: "Set me like a seal upon thy heart, love is as strong as death."

This thought enabled Victor to stay connected to that loving place within him that gave him strength and hope. By not blaming and placing emphasis on the external environment for his happiness, he was able to maintain a loving connection that kept him alive. After the war, he went on to become a world-renowned psychotherapist and author of the book *Man's Search for Meaning*, living until the age of ninety-two.

If you learn to observe your thoughts, like your feelings, without judgement, you will start to gain true mastery over your inner state. The first step in doing this is to separate yourself from your thoughts—you have thoughts, but are not the thought. This is the same concept as: you have feelings, but are not the feeling. Your true self is the stable, consistent observer of your thoughts and feelings. Living your life from your true self, rather than your fluctuating thoughts and feelings, is the key to happiness.

Nonjudgement is essential, because judging your thoughts complicates matters. Judgement introduces new thoughts. If the judgement is negative, it can lead to *catastrophizing* a thought process, or *mental looping*, rather than observing the presenting thought.

Catastrophizing is when a thought is allowed to escalate to increasingly more negative thoughts. For example, if you think, "Life is hard" and judge yourself badly for thinking this way, it creates an emotional charge around that thought. You could then build upon this with thoughts such as, "Things are getting more and more difficult all the time." "This year is going to be a lot worse than last year." On and on your thoughts can go, unconsciously creating increasing tension and stress in your mind and body.

However, you can stop the catastrophizing process by being aware of your original thought and neutralising it. Observe the first thought: "Life is hard" and see it as neither good nor bad. After observing the thought in a nonjudgemental way, you neutralize its power to create unwanted events in your life.

Mental looping is when a thought goes round and round and becomes stuck in your head. For example, if you think, "Life is hard," followed by, "I shouldn't think life is hard; I feel bad I think this way, but life is hard," and on it goes in an obsessive way of thinking! Again, lovingly observe the original thought, "Life is hard" and let it pass. If you catch yourself thinking obsessively, try to refocus your mind to a present experience, such as your breath, the noises around you, or the beauty of a nearby flower, to break the cycle of thought.

Consciously choosing not to think creates space and peace within you. This is what happens when you are completely absorbed by a breathtaking view, piece of art, focussed on a wonderful experience in sport or theatre, for example. When you are not thinking, you are in a state of *conscious awareness*, alert and immersed in the present moment—not thinking of the past or future. When you are present, you find yourself open to the beauty and joy that exists all around you. If your mind is obsessing about the past, or worrying about the future, you cut yourself off from this joy.

Setting aside time every day to quieten your mind, can add great value to the rest of your day. If you want to master your inner state, take time to learn and create this skill. Your mind is not supporting you when it is criticizing and "over thinking". It is possible to *train your mind for peace*, just as you can train your body to become fit. Initially, this takes effort and will, but after practice it becomes a natural way of being. It is well worth it to create a healthy and happy life.

If you think a thought regularly enough, it becomes a *belief.* Beliefs are one of the factors that determine the quality of your life. Often what you believe is created in your external world. When you are unaware of your thoughts or beliefs, they can control you. This can result in undesirable situations.

When you start to become aware of your thoughts and resulting beliefs you can begin to make choices around them. For example, you may be thinking: "It is only when I work really hard that I deserve to be successful," or "Life wasn't meant to be easy." *If you hold these beliefs consistently, that is how life will manifest for you.*

Learning to observe your thoughts or beliefs is one of the keys to increasing self-awareness. For example, I had an extremely busy period in my life recently. In one week, I was trying to finish my book, work in my kinesiology practice, had two birthday parties to organise, plus other social engagements. At the end of the last party I was thinking, "Phew, now this week is over I can get on with my life in a more relaxed fashion." At this exact instant, my five-year-old came home from a party with chicken pox. She was home recovering for two weeks. Fortunately I was able to put my work on hold and spent lots of quality time with her. The day she went back to school, I was intending to work, only to find, that I now had a cold. I was sick, just when I thought I had a chance to catch up! I caught myself thinking, "There is always something." In that moment I realised that as long as I was thinking "There is always something" that there would always be something! I was so grateful to become aware of this unconscious belief, as I could then change it, to one that supported my life. This awareness around my previously unconscious belief was enough to create change.

Your predominantly held beliefs add up to form an attitude. A person can have many beliefs, either positive or negative, about a situation. This person will have an attitude toward that situation based on the overall evaluation of her beliefs (Ajzen, 1991, 191–192). The attitudes that a person holds have a profound effect on the way that life manifests. For example, if you have the attitude, "Things work out well for me," this is how your life is likely to manifest. Again, becoming aware of the unconscious attitudes that don't support you—and changing them to ones that do—can help you to create the life you desire.

Living life with stress, anxiety, and depression indicate an agitated mind. Living with a restless mind can incrementally become a habit over time. The first step to change the habit is to be mindful of your thought processes. If you feel stressed or agitated in any way, observe your mind. It is likely it is thinking a lot. Develop ways to calm and centre your mind so that you control it, rather than it controlling you! For example, redirect your mind to your breath. Establish the intent that the breath will calm your mind. This can be done anytime, anywhere, the mind is restless. Another option is to choose not to think, and rest in awareness. In this state you will physically feel your mind relax as the tension from thinking is released from your head.

Once I stayed in a friend's apartment for a three-month period. My children were quite young at the time, and with hindsight I can see I was a lot less aware of my thought processes than I am now. I was highly anxious about the children having accidents and creating damage to the apartment. My children have always been naturally careful and have rarely had any accidents. However, during this period, silly little things would happen. I realize now, how my thoughts and stress contributed to this experience.

Recently I stayed in a friend's holiday home over Easter. At the beginning of the holiday, I set the intention that everything would go extremely well and that the house would be left in perfect order. I decided that, rather than stressing and worrying, we would all have a relaxing holiday. This is exactly what happened, and it reminded me of the power of thought!

Calming the chatter of your mind is a skill that is helpful in allowing you to understand the relationship between thoughts and feelings. A very busy mind can create disconnection between the mind and body, causing you to not know how you are feeling. It is important to have a direct link to your feelings and to understand them. Are your feelings triggered by your past, in the form of a reaction, that are resurfacing for healing (see chapter 5)? Are they trying to tell you something about the present? Calming the mind will enable you to begin to tell the difference. Misunderstood or misplaced feelings can be very dangerous. Feelings in themselves are fine, but when they are unconsciously acted upon, feelings, such as anger or jealousy, can seriously hurt the people around you. In these cases, it is the way that feelings *are dealt with* that are the problem.

Through awareness it is possible to develop control and not act inappropriately toward others. Adolf Hitler is an extreme example of someone who was not acting from a state of awareness. He was badly tortured by his father as a child. This resulted in a serious disconnection between his mind and body and his natural state of love. Rather than becoming conscious of the resulting thoughts and feelings, he acted them out, with terrifying results, due to his unconscious behaviour.

Mental resilience develops when you are not worrying about the past and future, but are instead, fully engaged in the present. When you do this, the energy that would have been consumed by catastrophizing and mental looping can be used to enjoy your life and for things such as creativity and the company of others. You will also find that when your mind is clear and calm, you are more likely to remember the things you need to do. Meditation is a very effective tool for calming your mind and developing mental resilience.

Meditating regularly will, over time, retrain a restless mind to one of peace. Meditation allows you to observe your thoughts and feelings without reaction and let them pass through your body. With practice you will go beyond thought and rest in a state of awareness. In this state you are fully present in the moment with a relaxed mind. The practical support section of this chapter gives a step-by-step approach to meditation.

A mantra, or commonly repeated word or phrase, is a very helpful meditation tool for creating a calm mind. Used in the East for thousands of years, mantras are becoming increasingly popular in the West. Mantras train the mind to become peaceful, by focussing the mind on one word that replaces negative thoughts.

A mantra can be a traditional Eastern word such as *Aum* (representing the sound of creation) or *So Ham* (translation: *I am that*) but any word that is meaningful to you, such as *calm*, *peace*, or *love,* is effective.

For example, if you are thinking, "Life is difficult, I am not doing things well enough, I am worried about the future," replace those thoughts with the mantra "Aum, Aum, Aum." This will give you a rest from your thoughts. Practiced often enough you will learn to observe and be aware of your thoughts. You can use your thoughts to manifest your life in a way that you would like, rather than having unconscious thinking create undesirable situations for you.

Initially you may be very resistant to meditating and not enjoy it at all—feeling restless and distracted. This is because when a new activity is introduced old ways of thinking are challenged. It takes a period of time for the brain to adjust. However, given time new neural connections in the brain are made and you will naturally feel more comfortable with the new activity. After consistently practicing meditation and working through your resistance, you may enjoy it and find it makes a positive difference to your life.

Often a mantra will automatically start playing in your head, overriding any previous negative thoughts. This is similar to your favourite song playing in your head, replacing any mental looping or catastrophizing. As you learn to calm your mind and still your thoughts, you will feel less anxious and stressed. Instead you will feel more relaxed and happy. As like attracts like, you will start to attract better experiences into your life.

When the mind is free of over-thinking and restlessness, you will be able to develop *mental clarity and resilience*. When you still your mind, you create space, rather than tension, within yourself. This space allows you to be receptive to your internal wisdom—also known as intuition (see chapter 6). It can be quite normal to obsess or worry about something. See this as a wonderful opportunity to transform your mind to one that is peaceful. Practice calming excessive thinking until your mind is still and quiet.

In difficult and testing circumstances, changing your perception will often allow you to feel better. A helpful question to ask yourself is: "How can I see this situation in a different way that does not cause me pain?" When I sold my home, it was initially very painful for me. However, over time, I have learned that it was part of my journey, taking me towards a greater, more permanent joy. When I reframed the experience in my mind it helped me to let go and move on with my life. In challenging circumstances ask yourself: "Is there another way of looking at this that will help me to feel better?" or, "I don't understand this right now but I'm sure I will in time." When you train your mind to support you in the most loving way possible, *peace is your reward.*

Acceptance of situations calms the mind, as it removes the emotional charge around them. Thoughts such as, "If I was better, this would not have happened" or "This undesirable situation occurred because I am a bad person," generally are of no help to you or anyone else. However, supportive thoughts such as: "Everything is going to be okay" or "I cannot understand the meaning of this right now, but I am sure at the right time I will understand," can make a positive difference. Such thoughts allow you to feel better and make it easier for you to cope during difficult times.

My experience is that when I practice thoughts of acceptance, internal pressure and resistance are released (like letting air out of a balloon) and I can relax and see my situation with more clarity. Examples of thoughts of acceptance could include:

1. I accept my past.
2. I accept my life is changing.
3. I accept that I did the best that I could with the skills that I had at the time.
4. I accept I don't like this situation.
5. I accept that I can/cannot do something about this situation.
6. I accept that I feel insecure right now.
7. I accept my relationship has changed.
8. I accept that I am a strong, capable person who can rebuild my life.

If things go wrong in life, it is never helpful to think you are wrong as a person. It may be helpful to gain some new skills, make changes, set boundaries, or look at things with a new loving perspective, as love is your true nature.

When you accept things as they are, your mind becomes calm. You are no longer coming from a defensive position. This allows you to access your intuition and operate your life from choice rather than being driven by unconscious thoughts and behaviours. Calming your mind is essential in creating a peaceful life.

Train your mind for peace.

practical support

- Calm your mind use the following meditation technique:
    - Sit comfortably on the floor in a cross-legged position or on a firm chair.
    - Sit on the sitting bones of your pelvis to ensure a straight spine (*if you lie down you could fall asleep and you need to be aware*).
    - Wear comfortable clothing, ensure you are warm, have an empty bladder, and are well hydrated.
    - Use a timer to time the session, anywhere from ten to thirty minutes.
    - If possible, meditate in an environment you love: the favourite part of your home, garden, or on a rock on the beach, for example.
        - Join your hands together in your lap.
        - Focus on your natural breathing in a relaxed way.
        - When and if thoughts and feelings arise, observe them without analysis or judgement. Let them go, like clouds passing through the sky. Return your focus on your breath throughout.
        - Some variations include:
            - Repeat a mantra to replace thoughts. When thoughts arise, take your focus back to the mantra.
            - Counting backwards from one hundred (good for a particularly busy mind).
            - Sit in a state of awareness beyond thought.
        - Practice meditation every day at about the same time.

- As you make more space in your inner world by calming your thoughts, your outer world will open up, and you will magically seem to have more time in your life.

Note: This is a formal description of meditation. However, meditation can be done anytime, anywhere—shopping, on the bus, or while you are walking, for example. Just focus on the breath and calm your mind and be very present to your surroundings. *With practice, life can become a moving meditation of joy!*

chapter five

reactions are like gold

reactions are designed to help you on your journey toward love and peace. Your world is like a mirror. What you see in others is usually a reflection of yourself. If you judge, find fault, and criticise others it can be helpful to ask if you are judging, finding fault, or criticising yourself. Generally, with loving awareness you will find some correlation. When you see only love in others, it is usually a sign you have found that beautiful loving place within yourself.

If you do react to someone, try to observe your feelings without judgement. The reaction and the resulting feelings are trying to tell you something *about yourself.* A reaction can unlock the door to greater awareness if you are able to take responsibility for your own feelings and not fall into the trap of blame. If you blame someone else for your feelings, you will not learn and grow from your experiences. This may result in a self-perpetuating cycle of reaction to others. This cycle is often painful and creates emotional unrest.

The key is to observe, work with, and understand your reactions. Over time, with practice, this process will help you to feel peaceful in most situations. You will know when you have successfully worked through a reaction when you put yourself in the same situation that you would have found stressful in the past, and are able to maintain your sense of peace.

Working with your reactions ultimately allows you to develop the skill of *emotional stability*: of being able to *respond rather than react* to a situation. This skill allows you to be the person you want to be in relationships, rather than feeling confused and out of control.

Understanding how the brain *automatically* creates a reaction can support you in being kind to yourself and others. Reactions are a survival response that is triggered in certain situations. A reaction is caused by the way *your brain perceives the issue.* This is due to your amygdala, a nut-shaped structure that sits at the base of your skull, in the middle of your brain. It assesses the environment for signs of danger through the senses: sight, hearing, taste, smell, and touch. The amygdala is part of the limbic system, the *survival centre*, associated with responses such as fear, rage, anger, pleasure, and fight or flight. Through emotional association to past events, the amygdala scans the environment for situations that create stress. Where it perceives danger, it will *react* in the way of flight or fight. For example, you could react to conflict by withdrawing, (flight) and be unable to find the right words to say. Alternatively you may attack aggressively (fight) and say things you don't mean.

This survival system is lightning-fast, providing an immediate subconscious reaction to an event. You know when a reaction has taken place when you feel some sort of emotional charge and generally don't feel very good. Words, such as *triggered, hooked in,* and *my buttons were pressed,* are often used to describe the event. Usually you feel strong physiological changes within your body, including:

1. Rapid heart rate
2. Faster breathing
3. Increased metabolism, which could make you feel shaky
4. A tight feeling in your stomach, due to your digestive system slowing down, and
5. A fuzzy head, due to the reduced function of your frontal brain and reasoning centres. (Corby 2003, 25)

These changes give your body more energy to allow you to run from perceived danger. An overactive survival response may have helped you in childhood, but rarely does in adulthood. As an adult, you can often be left feeling out of control, confused, and frustrated. A child's reasoning centres at the front of the brain are not fully developed until late adolescence (*Conference centres on adolescent brain development,* 2008). Therefore, particularly in early childhood, information is processed in a very emotional way. If a child grows up in an aggressive household, the amygdala may give the child signals to withdraw from a potentially dangerous situation (flight). This allows the child to draw less attention to him or herself and perhaps remain physically safe. The problem occurs when that person is in a similar situation as an adult. Any similarly aggressive situation, large or small, can trigger a flight reaction, as this pathway was programmed in the brain in the past and is now automatic. The adult will find him or herself reacting and withdrawing without wanting to. The reaction is often not proportional to the situation and leaves the adult feeling confused and out of control.

Part of the survival response is due to diminished frontal brain activity, which makes it harder to think clearly. Therefore, when the amygdala is overactive, we may feel that we *overreact to a stimulus* rather than providing a *measured response*.

When you react to a situation rather than respond, it is a good opportunity to develop greater awareness of your behaviour. It is common for people to blame others for their reactions, yet *another person cannot make you feel something.* A feeling is something that is going on inside *your* body. By taking full responsibility for your reaction, you can begin to step into your empowered self.

When you experience a reaction, the person you are dealing with is quite often reacting too. If so, it is often helpful to get away from the situation. This will give you both some space to sort out your reactions. Stay in touch with how you are feeling. Give the feeling a name. Perhaps you feel rejected. Ask yourself if you have ever felt this way before. Look back paying particular attention to the events of your life, prior to the age of six. This is when you experienced the world more emotionally as the frontal reasoning centres of your brain are not yet developed. However, do not look at this timeframe exclusively, as patterns of reaction can develop at any age.

If you can identify feeling rejected in certain situations in the past, you may notice a particular reactive pattern. For example, "I feel rejected if I *perceive* people are ignoring me and I can see that this has been a recurring pattern throughout my life." Awareness is often enough to release the old pattern. When new awareness is gained, there is often a physical sensation, or *shift*, in your body, signified by feeling better and a sense of expansion as you gain greater insight towards yourself.

As an adult, you can use your reasoning centres, which were not fully developed as a child, to help you *respond* to a situation. When you were growing up you may have been raised in a household where the parents were extremely busy and were unable to give you much attention. The reality was that you were ignored, which did result in you feeling rejected. *As an adult, however, you have choices*—you can choose love, rather than feeling rejected. You can use your reasoning centres to conclude that no one can make you feel rejected unless you let them. Adult reasoning can also help you to not make assumptions and give the other person the benefit of doubt. That is, by *doubting your thoughts*. Perhaps the other person was not ignoring you? Perhaps they were lost in their own thoughts, worried about how busy they are and how they were going to get it all done. They may have just received some bad news. You can change your reaction from rejection, by assuming the best of yourself and others. Ask yourself why would anyone reject you? Do not let your mind create answers that are false and not supportive of the wonderful individual that you are. Learn to own and observe your feelings of rejection and nourish them with *your* love. Learn to wrap yourself in the warm blanket of your love.

The reason to look at reactions is to understand what pain it is that you need to let go of. All pain is resistance to the natural flow of life. By looking at your reactions you are beginning to let go of pain and move to a place beyond suffering. Your mind is what created your reactional patterns in the first place. This process helps you to deconstruct those patterns allowing you to feel more in your natural state of peace, love and harmony.

To create a non-reactive or calm environment, it is helpful to stop thinking negative thoughts towards yourself. This process is to *bring love to places where there has been no love.* Start by observing any reactions within yourself lovingly. This love will then naturally flow on to your external environment. To prevent other people reacting to you, usually caused by their amygdala, endeavour not to say negative things to them. Allow people to experience their lives in their way, without criticism. Validate their feelings as they are. Validating your own feelings is very affirming and when you turn this process outwards, it helps to create an environment of *unconditional love.*

Training the mind to observe and nourish your reactions with love helps you to create a peaceful and loving inner world. This in turn helps you to develop more loving, fulfilling relationships in the world around you.

Bring love to places there has been no love.

practical support

- Work through the following steps when reacting:
    - Give yourself space from the person to whom you are reacting.
    - Stay with how you are feeling and name it: for example, *hurt*.
    - Establish whether you have felt this way before—is this feeling related to a behavioral pattern? For example, you may have repeatedly felt hurt when someone disagrees with you and now this has become a reactive (automatic) behavioural pattern.
    - If so, awareness is often sufficient to release the pattern. When new awareness is gained, there is often a shift in the body. This is often signified by recognition of the pattern, and feeling better as you expand and gain insight.
    - As an adult you can use your reasoning centres to *choose* your preferred response. You can doubt your thoughts. Perhaps the person's intention was not to hurt you. Perhaps the other person was having a bad day. Acknowledge and accept the feeling of hurt is *within you* for healing. Wrap the hurt feeling in a warm blanket of love. Observe and embrace it, and watch it dissipate with love.
    - Practise being the *observer* or *witness* of yourself in a situation, rather than "in" the situation. Clarity and insights will flow more easily, if you are less emotionally involved.
- Say only affirming things to yourself and others to calm amygdala reactions and *create an environment of unconditional love*. Speak from love rather than reaction to maintain relationships *and* get your needs met.

Note: Only focus on your reaction for a short period of time, until you develop the awareness around the reaction. See it as a gift to forgive yourself and others and then focus on the light in your life. Where focus goes energy flows.

chapter six

let your intuition be your guide

your intuition is your *internal guidance system* guiding you on a safe and happy journey throughout life! It is possible to spend a lifetime trying to follow something or someone to unlock the key to your happiness. It is common to search for happiness in another person or to think that happiness comes from somewhere *out there*. What people are looking for has actually been inside them the whole time! There have been many movies written with this underlying theme. Happiness *does* come from within.

Your intuition is always right for you—it is never wrong! It is the voice inside you that guides you safely on your journey throughout life—just like your own personal GPS. I have never met a person who has ever regretted following his or her intuition. However, I have met many people in my clinic who have regretted *not* following their intuition. Usually, they have let their head or *should* voice override what their intuition or heart is telling them.

When you put other people's opinions—the government, gurus, or other *experts*—ahead of what you want to do, you are not listening to your intuition. Alternatively, you may believe it is your intuition that you are listening to when it is actually fear. If you are saying, "I should do this, or that," usually it is fear-based, perhaps to keep other people happy, to maintain appearances, or to be liked, for example.

When you say, "This is what I really want to do," or "I'd love to do that," it is usually coming from your intuition. If it is the right decision for you, generally it is the right decision for everyone around you. Doing what is right for you sets a good example for everyone else to do the same. This is also referred to as *modelling.* The world would be a very happy place if everyone did what made him or her happy. When you are happy, generally you are more giving, supportive, and kind.

It is very difficult to be in tune with your intuition if you are unable to access your feelings and let them flow. Your feelings are one of the ways in which your intuition speaks to you. For example, your intuition lets you know when something *feels bad* or when something makes you *truly happy* (see chapter 3). Being in tune with your body is also critical. When you have a *gut feeling* about a situation, it is your intuition at work.

One of the most critical aspects of listening to your intuition is to be able to quieten your mind. If your mind is too busy or stressed, it does not allow space for you to hear what your intuition is telling you. When you rush from one thing to the next, over long periods of time, you can become disconnected from your intuition. This disconnection is leading to widespread mental and physical disease in our world today.

A lot of the time your body may be telling you to slow down, so that you can listen to your intuition and make the right decision. When you are too busy to listen, sometimes the body makes you sick, forcing you to stop and listen. For some people it is not until they are very, very sick that they are willing to listen and act on what their intuition is telling them.

When you provide space in your life to listen and act on your intuition, you will find that your life starts to flow. Your intuition is always guiding you toward health and happiness. Sometimes people are afraid that if they are not busy all the time, things are going to fall apart. In fact the opposite is true. It is quite common that when you start listening to your intuition, your life becomes solid and secure. This is because it is built on a solid foundation of love—love of doing what is right for you. When you make the shift and begin to live in this way, you often find you have more time, are more relaxed and in tune with yourself, and able to enjoy your life in an authentic way.

The more relaxed you are the more in tune you will be with your intuition. Do not look at being relaxed as a luxury or as something you do on the weekend. *See living your life in a relaxed way as essential to creating a happy life.* Set some time aside, preferably at the beginning of the day, to consciously relax. A walk in nature or meditation is ideal for this. This will set you up to feel your best at the beginning of the day, allowing you to cope more easily with any challenges that may come your way. The more relaxed you are, the more likely you are to know what is right for you. As a result you will become *more* productive in a way that is tailor-made for your happiness.

It is easier to access your intuition when you feel emotionally stable. Emotional stability develops when you are able to observe your problems like a witness rather than being *in* the problem. Rather than getting caught up in your emotions, calm yourself by settling your thoughts in a way that works for you—by focussing on your breath, playing sport, gardening, or taking a walk in nature, for example. This will allow you to look at the situation objectively and allow your intuition to give you the answer to what you would like to know. When you are less absorbed in your emotional issues, you tend to live your life from a more benevolent state—one where you want to be kind and of service to others. This is because instead of being consumed by the drama your mind is creating, you use that energy to be creative and of service.

The four main aspects of intuition are:

1. **Know** your intuition. Learn to be aware of it. It may speak to you in words through your inner voice, or you may feel it in terms of sensations in your body such as your gut feeling and/or goose bumps. Be mindful of the difference between *a reaction*, where your body's survival system is telling you that something from your past needs healing (see chapter 5), and *a response*, where your intuition is guiding you.

2. **Trust** your intuition. When you are in touch with your intuition, *trust* that it is right for you. Sometimes you may be aware of your intuition but not trust it. It is your guidance system, personally designed to take care of you—for life. Have faith in yourself and trust your intuition.

3. **Act** on your intuition. Do what your intuition tells you and your life will begin to flow. If you don't take action, you may find yourself stuck in the same old situation, feeling frustrated. When you act on your intuition, happiness is one of the benefits of its guidance.

4. **Speak** from your intuition. Your intuition is *what is true for you* or *your truth*. Your intuition comes from your heart—a loving place. When you speak your

truth, the quality of your life improves, as you are congruent in what you think, feel, and say. Ideally, you will process your emotions as you go (rather than repress or suppress them) and develop the skills to say how you feel in an appropriate way in the moment (see practical support, chapter 10). To do this effectively you have to know you are responding rather than reacting to events (see chapter 5). Unless you are able to say what is important to you, it is easy to be misunderstood by others and possibly find yourself in situations that are not right for you.

Be proactive and consciously go out and create the life you want, guided by your intuition. If you sit back and wait for things to happen without your input, you could be waiting for a long time! Your intuition will tell you when to act and when to hold back; when you are doing too much and when you need to rest; what is beneficial to you and what is not. By listening to your intuition, you'll know moment to moment, what is right for you. It has the ability to guide you through even the most difficult challenges you may face. Rather than a life based on stress and pressure, your intuition has the ability to facilitate your life unfolding in a natural, flowing way.

Your intuition is always right for you.

practical support

- Create space in your life and quieten your mind so you can hear your intuition. Develop an awareness of the language of your thoughts. Ask yourself: "Is it the *should* voice (fear/guilt) or the *I'd love to* voice (intuition) that is speaking to me?"

- Learn to observe your problem like a witness rather than be *in* the problem. This helps to develop emotional stability, which allows you to access your intuition. Replay your problem out in front of you, like you are watching yourself on the television.

- Calm your mind by taking a walk in nature, meditate, or play sports, for example. With a calm mind you are more easily able to access your intuition and receive the custom made guidance for you!

chapter seven

connecting to the greatest power source on earth

there is a field of energy that is responsible for all of creation. Energy is everywhere and it is what makes you feel good and alive. When you consciously connect to this energy field, you are likely to feel more connected to other people, as we are all made from the same energy. When you feel disconnected from this energy source, usually by the thoughts you create, it is more likely that you will feel disconnected from the true beauty that is you!

Energy is your power source. You cannot lift your arm without energy, in fact, without energy you would not exist. Where there is no energy, there is no life. Energy is something you *experience—it is something you feel*. The stronger your energy or life force usually the more happy, joyous, and healthy you feel.

Energy has been referred to in many ways throughout history, including Chi and Prana. Some of the spiritual terms used to describe energy include God, Love, Tao, Spirit, the Matrix, Divine Healing Intelligence and the Universal Intelligence Field.

Previously, understanding and working with energy has been seen by many as something that has been available only to gurus, enlightened masters or other forms of elevated spiritual beings. However, the year 2000 marked a new era, which has been referred to as "The Golden Age". This age signifies a new era in history where people are becoming more aware of and in tune with energy.

The etheric body is the energy template for living beings. It is a thin invisible body that runs through, and extends a few cm past, the physical body. The etheric body sustains and supports the physical body. It appears as an energy matrix made up of meridians and charkas and allows energy to flow through the body. Meridians and charkas connect to and nourish all the major organs, glands and nerves in the physical body.

All life forms including plants and animals have an etheric body. Nothing physical can be alive without an etheric body as it feeds the physical with energy that is vital for its health and survival. When your meridians and charkas are open and flowing with energy you feel energetic and alive. When energy blockages occur in your etheric body you do not feel in an optimum state of health and well-being. The following is an overview of the major energy centers:

1. **Meridians:** Like veins carry blood around your body, the meridians transport energy. The flow of the meridian energy pathways is as critical as the flow of blood. *Where there is no energy, there is no life.* The meridian system brings vitality and balance, removes blockages, adjusts metabolism, and determines the speed and form of cellular change. Meridians affect every organ and every physiological system, including the immune, nervous, endocrine, circulatory, respiratory, digestive, skeletal, muscular, and lymphatic systems. Each system is fed by at least one meridian. If a meridian's energy is obstructed or unregulated, the system it feeds is jeopardized. The meridians include fourteen tangible channels that carry energy into, through, and out of your body. Your meridian pathways also connect hundreds of tiny, distinct reservoirs of heat and electromagnetic energy along the surface of the skin. These are your acupuncture points, and they can be stimulated with needles or physical pressure to release or redistribute energy along the meridian pathway.

2. **Chakras:** The word chakra translates from the Sanskrit as disk, vortex, or wheel. The chakras are concentrated centers of energy. Each major chakra in the human body is a center of swirling energy positioned at one of seven points, from the base of your spine to the top of your head. Each chakra supplies energy to specific organs, corresponds to a distinct aspect of your personality, and resonates with one of seven universal principles. The base chakra relates to survival, the sacral chakra to creativity, the solar plexus chakra to identity, the heart chakra to love, the throat chakra to expression, the brow chakra to comprehension, and the crown chakra relates to transcendence. Your chakras also code your experiences in their energies, just as memories are chemically coded in your neurons. An imprint of every emotionally significant event

you have experienced is recorded in your chakra energies.

3. **Auras:** Your aura is a multi-layered shell of energy that emanates from your body and interacts with the energies of your environment. Technology has been developed so that auras can now be videoed and analysed in real time. Auras are referred to by scientists as "biofields". The aura is a two-way circuit that brings in energy from the environment to your chakras and that sends energy from your chakras outward. When you feel happy, attractive and spirited, your aura may fill an entire room. When you are sad, despondent, and somber, your aura is more closed, forming an energetic shell that isolates you from the world.

Understanding the etheric body is helpful in understanding energy and how it flows through your physical body. Feelings and thoughts can have an energetic charge around them that effects energy flowing freely through your meridians, charkas and auras. These energetic centers flow freely when thoughts and feelings are able to pass through the body in a neutral way. That is why it is helpful to be able to develop the ability to observe your feelings neutrally (i.e. without an emotional charge or judgment) and let them flow. As discussed previously, meditation can be a helpful tool to develop this skill, just as exercising helps to keep your body fit. Understanding your inner world in terms of thoughts and feelings and how it affects your life-force helps you maintain your health and well-being.

Physicist and Nobel Prize winner Max Planck is considered to be the founder of quantum physics. During the first half of the twentieth century, he discovered that life-force energy and spiritual energy is the same thing—a huge, intelligent, creative all-knowing energy field.

Another way to see it is that the mind and body are the first and second dimensions, and energy—also referred to as spirit—is the third dimension. When your mind and body are working together (see chapters 3 and 4), you usually feel more energised.

When you consciously access the third dimension, the true magic of life takes place. By consciously tapping into the power of energy or spirit or love, you are more likely to live your life to your full potential. This is because it is like plugging into a giant source of energy that is always there to support you. This is possible for anyone. Stilling the restlessness of the mind and becoming fully engaged in the moment are the keys to connecting to your energy source.

When you quieten your mind you are more able to be aware or *present* to what is going on around you. This is because a still mind allows your attention to be focused on Gods beauty that is everywhere.

Ken Carey describes the presence of God so beautifully in the following passage:

> *I would rather slip up beside you as you work in the garden, or look in your eyes and smile as I give you your change. I would rather wash your windows carefully, be courteous when you ask for direction. I would rather appear to you as a simple man, woman or child, simply being, enjoying being, taking time for the little things. Look for me, then in these ways. See me in everyone you meet, whether they recognize my Presence or whether they yet sleep. See me in all. For I am there, eternally, behind every pair of eyes.* (Carey, 1985, 5)

God's presence can be witnessed in all forms of life. Presence is in the moments that people take to enjoy their life. Presence can be found equally in big *magic* moments, such as the sunset in a foreign country that takes your breath away, and also in the *joy of everyday experience.* Walking your child to school can be totally joyful; the exchange of kind words or deeds with a complete stranger can be joyful. Watching a butterfly flit from leaf to leaf can be a beautiful experience.

The opportunity to witness God abounds. All you have to do is be aware and notice. Recently on a trip to the park with my five-year-old daughter, Scarlett, I consciously focussed on being present. I listened to every word she said. I did not let my mind take over with thoughts about the past or future, which would take me away from the joy of being with her. The result was that we had the most wonderful afternoon. We noticed a baby lorikeet on the ground and the beauty of the magnificent Morton Bay fig trees by the beach. Our afternoon tea was delicious, and swinging Scarlett on the swing was pure bliss. Nothing had changed in the environment, only my perception. I was fully engaged in the present moment, and this allowed me to access the joy that is inherent in all of us. Scarlett was effortlessly present and joyful, as children often tend to be.

Quietening your mind and going beyond thought allows you to hear your intuition, your internal wisdom. This is your direct line to the Universal Intelligence Field or God. *Your intuition is actually God talking to you*—that is why your intuition is never, ever wrong! When you listen to your intuition, you are accessing your inherent wisdom, your source of power.

The intelligence of your intuition knows everything. Ask your intuition what it is you'd like to know. If it does not provide the answer directly, it will guide you to the correct course, person, or book, or give you the answer through your dreams, for example.

When your thoughts are consumed with the past or future, you may find it difficult to connect to your intuition. Just like static can prevent clear transmission from the radio station. When you are fully focussed on the present moment and free from restless thoughts, it is easier to hear what your intuition is saying.

Being aware and present to energy or God or love can help you to create a life that is far more amazing than what you can create alone. When you create your life by working with source energy, it is known as *co-creation*. Source energy loves by nature, so if you create a life based on love rather than fear it makes sense that you will feel happier and more content. Love feels better in your body than fear.

Engaging wholeheartedly in work that you love, helps you to create this experience. Many great artists and writers openly attribute their work as an expression of co-creation with God. It is common for artists to say that it is God's energy that flows though them and is manifested in their work—they are the conduit to this manifestation.

Michelangelo's creation of the Sistine Chapel is an inspiring example of what a single man can achieve when co-creating with God. During his lifetime Michelangelo was a sculptor, painter, and architect. He produced works such as the Statue of David, the Sistine Chapel frescos, and was the architect of the Medici Chapel. To be a highly accomplished sculptor, painter, or architect is amazing in itself, but the fact he was a master in *all three* areas is truly awe-inspiring.

Michelangelo believed that his art was an expression of God, as he expressed in the following poem:

> *Whatever beauty here on earth is seen,*
> *To meet the longing and perceptive eye,*
> *Is semblance of that source divine,*
> *From whence we all come.*
> *In this alone we catch a glimpse of Heaven.*
> ~ Michelangelo

Connecting to divine inspiration is possible for anybody. To do this you need to find that space of awareness within you that is beyond thought. Meditation can be helpful in this process. When you go beyond the chatter of your mind, you are generally able to form a direct connection with your energy source or God. Creativity innately comes from this source of inspiration. In fact the definition of inspiration is *inspired by spirit*.

I once committed to create thirty pieces of art for a local solo art exhibition. I had three months to complete the work. I felt time pressured but was lucky enough to have the support of my family to help look after my young children. Most of the work was created in peace and quiet while I was alone. However, the last piece I did during a painting day with my children, who were also creating their own masterpieces! We were having such fun together and really enjoying the process. On that afternoon I produced by far my best work: a small abstract piece I named *Heart*, which I used as the title piece for the exhibition. The work flowed effortlessly as I was not consumed by my mind. It was produced in my natural, loving, joyous state, surrounded by the love of my children.

Although meditation can be a helpful tool, long hours of meditation and/or a devotional lifestyle are not required to feel inspired or connected to God. Opportunities to learn how create a calm mind and connect to your powerful energy source are everywhere. For example:

1. Give your full attention to someone when they are talking to you. If you find your mind wandering from the conversation, consciously bring your attention back to them and really listen.

2. Fully concentrate on your driving. If you are driving your car on *automatic pilot,* bring yourself back to what you are doing in the present moment.

3. Give your full attention to brushing your teeth. If your mind wanders, bring it back and focus on cleaning your teeth so they sparkle!

When you start to tune your mind to the present moment, you will bring a sense of quality and peace into your life. Rather than doing things by half measure, things will be done well. Learning to focus the mind is an important step in learning to let the mind know it is you who is in control. *This ultimately will enable you to transcend the suffering it can create.* With a clear mind you will begin to notice the natural order and beauty of life. Next time you look at a tree, *really look at it* and you will appreciate how beautiful it is. Next time you are with someone, *give him or her your full attention,* without judgement, and you will notice his or her inherent beauty.

When you are fully present, you are more aware and intuitive. This allows you to feel a *genuine* connection with people, beyond the intellectual concept. In an intuitive state, you actually embody compassion, love, and kindness towards yourself and others. You just *know things* and tune into other people when they are tuning into you. For example, you may telephone someone just as he or she is telephoning you.

Presence allows you to be in conscious contact with God— connecting you to the power of creation and the field of unlimited possibilities. To be truly empowered and to create the life you desire, once you are in tune with God or the Universal Intelligence Field, you need to take action in relation to what you are hearing.

This may mean taking a course, changing jobs, finding a new relationship, or developing new skills.

It is possible for anyone to develop presence and be in conscious contact with God. In fact it is very easy because it is the most natural thing in the world (*A Course in Miracles*, 1975, 64). Our beliefs determine our reality. If we think something will be hard, it is hard. If we think it is easy, it will be. For thousands of years, many people have had us believe that it is difficult for us to reach God, or that you have to go through a *series of steps*, follow a specific person, that it is only for a chosen few, or if you are special. If you believe this, then that is how it will be for you. However, if you believe that God is always with you and can be contacted anytime, anywhere, just by being in touch with your intuition, that will be your experience.

Sometimes another voice inside you, known as your ego or mind (more on ego in chapter 13), will try to convince you that you'll never be connected to God, that it's too hard, or that God is not real. If this is so, acknowledge the resistance, but have faith and trust it is entirely possible to embody God. *In fact, you are God* as you are made from the same energy. God or love is within you and surrounds you everywhere all the time. Enlightenment can be described like a bird searching for the sky while it is flying in it! You do not need to search for God when you already are God. Enlightenment is not a matter of going on a journey to find love but more like opening up and acknowledging the love that you already are. *Be open to love!*

I welcomed in the 2004 New Year with my family on the foreshore of Sydney Harbour. It was a magic night. It was something I'd always wanted to do. We got a fantastic position with uninterrupted views of the fireworks. The sunset was exquisite and the fireworks spectacular (including a huge red heart lighting up Sydney's Harbour Bridge); the atmosphere from the crowds was alive and full of New Year's spirit. I felt completely blissful and contented and later described the whole experience as *Heaven on Earth.* I was fully absorbed in the moment enjoying the company of my husband and three children.

I said during that night to my husband, that my goal one day is to become enlightened. I then proceeded on a six-year journey *looking for enlightenment.* What my journey has taught me is that my 2004 New Year's Eve experience is what enlightenment is all about. Enlightenment is not something that you find or get, but rather something that is around you all the time. You just have to be open to it.

Enlightenment is everywhere and when we begin to change our perception, we begin to *see*. See with a heart of love, rather than a mind of judgement and fear. Now that I have discovered that peace is all in my perception, I have trained myself to feel contented, even during the busiest traffic! I can't change the traffic, so I might as well enjoy it!

Tap into the present to experience the joy and miracle of life. Rather than seeing the energy field as a miraculous source of power *out there*, recognise that you are made up of exactly the same energy. *You are the same miracle, the same love.* Love is everywhere, all the time.

Be open to love.

practical support

- Train yourself to focus on the present moment. Practice by listening fully to others. Give your full attention to everyday tasks such as: chopping vegetables, driving the car, or cleaning your teeth. This brings quality and satisfaction to the moment you are in.

- In stressful situations, focus on your breath to help quieten your mind so you can "hear" your intuition.

- When you need guidance, ask God. You may be given the answer directly though your intuition. Alternatively, you may be guided to a book, course, or person that will help you with what you'd like to know, for example.

- Be open to solutions that you may not have thought of. God often gives back to you in ways better than you could have imagined! The key is to *let go of your preconceived ideas and remain open!*

- Be aware that God or love rests in you and that you rest in love or God at all times. Division is created by the mind. You are love—there is no difference.

chapter eight

live your life
on purpose

experience the joy of creating your life as an expression of what you love to do. Joy is something that can be felt in the present moment rather than struggling for years on end to *then* enjoy the fruits of your labour. Joy is available to anyone, anywhere, not only when you are rich, have the right partner, are retired, or have *time* to enjoy your life—which is sometimes what the mind will try to tell you!

Find out what it is that you love to do and what is meaningful to you. What gets you enthusiastically wanting to get out of bed every day? Allow yourself to express your talents through your work, and you will be living your life on purpose. You may need to develop your talents into skills through training; however, if it is what you love to do, you will find it a joyful part of the journey. Expressing your gifts and talents can be a great source of joy and happiness. *Do what makes your soul sing.*

If your passion is to be a musician but you decide to be a lawyer because it pays more, you may feel inside that you are *off course* in some way. This will be indicated by feelings of dissatisfaction. You may develop the skills to be a lawyer and find some interest in the profession, but if it is not your passion, what you love to do, you are always going to feel (and this can be buried very deeply) that something is wrong or missing.

Chances are that if you really want to be a musician and it is your true purpose in life, you could be very good at your profession and be paid more than a lawyer. However, for people who are truly on purpose in life, the money is just a bonus. When you are on purpose, you experience a deep sense of fulfilment that can be measured in ways other than money.

Teachers, who love sharing their knowledge and the company of children, are likely to be living their life on purpose. They may not be the most highly paid in the community, but know the internal happiness that comes from doing what they love. Similarly if you want to be a stockbroker but instead take up gardening, you may not feel deeply fulfilled by your work. Career compromise can occur for reasons such as: financial reward, not feeling good enough, or following someone else's wishes instead of what you want to do.

Life will always give you clues if you are not on track with your true purpose. This may feel like slight discomfort or unhappiness. In the workplace, you may feel like a *square peg in a round hole*. Time at work drags on; you look forward to lunch. These are all signals that you are not living your life on purpose.

You can use these signs as opportunities to find out what it is that you love to do. It may often be helpful to look at what brought you joy and happiness as a child. Try to think back to before you were five and what naturally captured your interest. There are many books, internet sites, sophisticated testing systems, and life coaches that can help you discover what you love to do, if you can't work it out. It can be helpful to ask: "What am I really enthusiastic about? What inspires me?"

Unfortunately, signs that you are not on track with your life's purpose can easily be ignored. The body relentlessly gives you signals until you listen. If you don't listen when the signals are small, they can present themselves as physical symptoms until you take notice. For example, Stage 2 stress signals such as sinus problems, colds, or poor eyesight. At this stage you could ask yourself, "Am I doing what I truly love in my life?" If not, it is a great opportunity to take responsibility for your happiness and start to develop a plan.

Due to your current commitments, it may not be possible to change your profession quickly. However, it is entirely possible to work towards doing what you love to do. When you have tapped into your life's purpose, you will have the energy and find the means to make it happen. You will be naturally excited and develop creative ways to do the work that you enjoy. If you are not excited and enthusiastic about your job most of the time, it is a sign *you are in the wrong job for you!*

It can be easy to compromise on your life's purpose for your children or partner, for example. Generally, however, by being the best you can be, you encourage and allow others around you to shine. There is *always* a way to have it all, if that is what you want—the desire has to come from you. It may involve a long-term plan and a changeover period, but creating the life you want is always worth it. A period of trial and error may follow as you experiment with different things on your path of discovery. This could take months or years. However, being true to you is the important thing. Give yourself the opportunities to move towards living your life on purpose.

You will know when you are working in the right area, because most of the time you will feel happy. Work will seem to flow, and you will feel energized at the end of the day. In fact, it is unlikely to feel like work at all, but more like play. Feeling energized and happy when you have finished work indicates you are in the right place for you!

During my thirties I was employed as a human resources manager in a large corporation and then later in another company as a homewares buyer. Although I did the jobs to the best of my ability, I found myself constantly looking at my watch and looking forward to lunch. I would feel very tired and de-energised at the end of the day. Both of these positions had a large administration component, which is not in line with my natural skills and talents. I ended up leaving both these jobs after a mere six-month period when I realised that they were not the right jobs for me.

When I ran my own businesses, the days would fly by. I often forgot about having lunch, as I was so engrossed in what I was doing. I had many difficult times in both businesses, but my underlying belief in my work enabled me to move through the challenges. In business if you experience difficult financial times you may have no choice but to work your way through them. If possible, learn and implement the strategies to get the business in a solid financial position, and then reassess if it is the business that is best suited to you. I learned from my experiences that work where I was involved in leadership and creativity was better suited to my natural interests. I feel happier and more fulfilled when I am engaged in these areas as a result.

Living your true purpose may involve some sacrifice in terms of time and money, in the short run. You may have to engage in work that is not your preference while you study, for example, but if you are living on purpose it makes it all worthwhile. Gandhi had to endure unpleasant situations during his lifetime. His sense of purpose sustained him through the challenging times.

Ensure that you give yourself every opportunity when it comes to living your life on purpose. Find out what makes your soul sing and do it!

Do what makes your soul sing.

practical support

- Write out a list of things that nourish your soul in terms of career, relationships, finances, health, and spiritual matters. What is it that you love to do and you find easy? What makes you feel enthusiastic and inspired? Journaling can be a fantastic tool to give you clarity. Don't think—just write.
- Life coaches, internet sites with career testing questionnaires, and career guidance books can be helpful tools in helping you to discover what it is you love to do.

chapter nine

gratitude, optimism and kindness

gratitude, optimism, and kindness are integral in living a life of peace, joy, and happiness. When you express gratitude, optimism, and kindness, it generates a beautiful energy that shines from you. It feels good to share gratitude, optimism, and kindness. Not for reward or from expectation, but because you want to share the joy you feel inside.

As well as being able to give love in terms of gratitude and kindness, it is equally important to allow yourself to receive love. Dr's Harville Hendrix and Helen LaKelly Hunt are internationally renowned relationship therapists. Through their work they discovered that many people find it easier to give love rather that receive it. Maintaining a natural balance in giving and receiving love is important in order to feel happy. Softening and opening your heart is the key.

Finding it more difficult to receive love than give love can relate to having had a traumatic experience. A trauma can make you nervous about letting people get too close to you in case you get hurt. By looking at the trauma (see chapters 2 and 14), making peace with it and forgiving those involved can be helpful in beginning to trust in love again. Forgiveness, compassion, and understanding help to melt away defences and let you feel more open and safe in receiving love.

It has been scientifically proven that expressing gratitude just once a week for ten minutes over a six-month period substantially increases the level of your happiness (Boehm and Lyubormirsky, 2009, 673). You can express gratitude in a journal or *on the go* as events occur in your life. There are many ways to express gratitude. You can say thank you to people directly, pick up the phone, write a letter, send an email, or give someone a hug, for example—the possibilities are endless. And they make you *both* feel good. *Gratitude and happiness go hand in hand.* When you feel loving towards your friend, for example, you automatically feel grateful that they are in your life. It is impossible to feel grateful and unhappy at the same time.

The energy of transformation is one of hope and love. By accepting where we are in our lives, while taking positive steps to achieve our goals with an optimistic view, anything becomes possible. Where focus goes, energy flows.

Gratitude, optimism, and kindness are the greatest gifts you can give to yourself and others. Feeling ungrateful towards life drains your energy and causes pain, as you resist what is already there. When you accept yourself as you are, you can start to relax and focus on reframing situations to support you in the best possible way. For example, you may be unhappy with your height, but this is a predetermined factor that is easier to accept than struggle against. However, you can change the way you think about your height. *Thinking is something you have complete control over.* It is possible to find positive aspects in relation to being either tall or short. When you accept the things you can't change and are grateful for what you have, you keep your energy flowing rather than creating resistance and pain around a situation.

Gratitude can bring a whole new meaning to a situation. Gratitude can turn mistakes into opportunities, that create understanding and help you to learn and grow. It can turn sorrow into hope; pain into love. When you relook at a situation that previously made you insecure and fearful through the eyes of compassion and kindness your heart softens—opening and allowing you to flow with life in a more joyful way.

Gratitude, optimism, and kindness are expressions of positive energy and love. Positive energy attracts positive situations into your life, as like attracts like. Expressing love towards others and yourself allows you to embrace the natural joy of life.

Gratitude and happiness go hand in hand.

practical support

- Write down all the things that you are grateful for in terms of life lessons. What did you see as difficult and painful at the time, but now you understand the deeper meaning and appreciate the growth it bought you.
- Write an optimistic story about your future, covering all levels of your life, such as relationships, career, finance, spirituality, and health.
- Write down all the things you love about yourself.
- Write down things you love about someone else and *give it to them.*
- Do kind things for others *and learn to love people as they are.*

I find that when something great happens to me, my body is filled with a wave of gratitude, I automatically say thank you to God, who I believe co-creates my life. I call this "gratitude on the go."

chapter ten

the joy of consciously relating

relationships can create the greatest joy or the greatest pain—including the relationship you have with yourself! When you are aware of your behaviours, it is easier to create the relationships you want. This is because awareness allows you to understand your behavioural patterns rather than being unconsciously driven by them.

Emotional issues arising from relationships can become all consuming, drain you of energy, and take you away from your peace. However, becoming more conscious or aware of your behaviours and changing your perspective allows you to develop deep and loving relationships.

Being conscious involves observing your thoughts and feelings rather than being swept away by them. This *new awareness allows you to grow*, and make choices in your life that make you happy. As you become more conscious it helps the quality of your relationships improve because you have the skills to deal with your reactions and conflict in a healthy way. Conflict can be an opportunity to bring you closer together, and create greater understanding, if it is dealt with in a constructive way.

A conscious person respects the choices of others. People no longer have to be a certain way around you for you to be happy— you are in touch with your internal happiness system. It is freeing for everyone when you respect others and *let them experience life in their way.* You are responsible for experiencing your life in a way that makes you happy. If someone wants your advice, it is likely they will ask for it. Unsolicited advice is generally unwelcome as it gives the unspoken message, *I know better than you.*

To be in touch with your internal happiness system you need to go beyond the chatter of your mind to a place where you *feel* loving. When you experience yourself as the loving individual you are, you will recognise that same love in other people. When you see the best in yourself, you see the best in others. For example, if you constantly think guilty thoughts (even unconsciously), guilt will manifest in your relationships. However, if you go beyond those thoughts, recognising that guilty thoughts are not who you are, they are just thoughts or a trick of the mind, you will connect to the *real you,* which is love. You can then choose to base your relationships on love rather than guilt. Remain very present in the relationship rather than ruminating over old issues, or worrying about the future, and watch the quality of your relationship skyrocket!

In a conscious relationship, you take full responsibility for your feelings. For example, if you constantly feel fear around a particular person, they are not making you fearful—fearful feelings are being activated in you. It is empowering to take responsibility for those fearful feelings and understand why they are occurring. This person may remind you of another fearful situation. It may be your intuition telling you this is not the right situation for you. Gaining insight into your behavioural patterns allows you to make choices that enable you to maintain loving connections with others.

In a conscious relationship you give the people around you the space and support to take responsibility for exploring their own feelings. You also have the ability to draw clear boundaries. You are able to be empathetic without taking on their feelings, which don't belong to you.

When consciously relating, you develop the skills to manage your energy. Observing and accepting your feelings and acting on them from choice rather than reacting, helps you to feel emotionally stable. An emotionally stable person is usually more fun to be around. When you don't take things personally and instead stay in the moment, you will be more in tune with people and have wisdom to share.

In a conscious relationship, when issues do arise, you do not gossip. There is a difference between gossiping and using someone you trust as a sounding board to help you gain insight. If a conflict arises, it is important to take responsibility and gain clarity around your feelings. *Then* if it still seems necessary, get together with the other person and discuss the issue. Once you have sorted out your feelings, you may see things differently and no longer need to discuss the situation.

To communicate in times of conflict:

1. Recognise and address conflict in the early phases when it is easier to resolve.

2. Deal with conflict if possible by sitting down and discussing it in person. Messages sent by email and text messages can be easily misunderstood further escalating the situation. GOLDEN RULE: Speak to someone directly to sort out conflict. However, it is constructive to praise someone in writing.

3. Manage your own emotions by breathing, taking a walk in the park for example, until you calm down and work out what is really going on for you.

4. Determine if you are reacting to the situation. If you are, sort out your reaction independently before talking to the person involved (see chapter 5).

5. Listening empathetically and acknowledge how the other person feels *before* you share how you are feeling. When they have been heard it allows them to hear you as their emotions have been diffused. *Seek first to understand and then to be understood.* (Covey, 1989, 235)

6. Take responsibility for your feelings. Say how *you* feel without criticizing or blaming the other person. To avoid the person feeling attacked and becoming defensive (escalating the conflict), *focus on your feelings rather than on their behaviour.* Be open, honest, and communicate only when you are ready to do so from a loving perspective. If your fears or concerns are spoken from a loving place, the other person is more likely to hear you.

7. After stating how you feel, it can be helpful to brainstorm ideas. This will help you both come to a natural solution that is more likely to meet both your needs. Be light about it. This process can even be fun! Do not focus on the outcome, but remain open to a range of possibilities (stay in your intuitive space, see chapter 6).

Expanding your consciousness does require some effort, in terms of training your mind to be peaceful rather than reactive. However, the more conscious and peaceful you become, the more you are able to rise above mental and physical suffering—consciousness is your ticket to freedom, joy, and bliss.

Table 2: Characteristics of Conscious vs. Unconscious Relationships

Unconscious relationships	Conscious relationships
Blame others	**Responsibility** for self
Gossip	**Trust**
Little or no growth	**Growth** due to new awareness
Stuck in **confusion**	Confusion leading to **clarity**
Unable to **ask** for **support**	**Ask for support** when needed
Need **instant fix** when uncomfortable with feelings	**Able to sit with uncomfortable feelings**
Unclear boundaries	**Defined boundaries**
React to others	**Respond** to others
Unstable	**Stable**
Look for **others to make them feel better**	Skills to **make self feel better**
Shallow	**Deep connection**
Heavy energy	**Light** and **fun** energy
Stagnant: stuck energy	**Evolving:** fresh and alive
Fear-based	Based on **love**

- Develop the ability to be light and easy in your relationships. If possible, discuss issues in a light and easy way as they come up. John Gottman, relationship expert and co-founder of the Gottman Institute, has found that people who have mastered successful relationships bring up problems gently and without blame (Gottman's Marriage Tips 101, 2004). They are able to express what they feel and what they need *gently. Discussions invariably end on the same note as they begin* (John Gottman, 2004).

- The more conscious and aware you are of your thoughts and feelings, the more present you are able to be with others. When you are with someone, give him or her your full attention, rather than letting the mind taking you elsewhere. You will hear what they are saying and be able to give meaningful responses. *Deeply listening without judgement is one of the kindest gifts you can give.* Examining and being aware of the way *you* are in your relationship allows you to make choices around it. Relating to others from love brings deeper understanding and connection.

New awareness allows you to grow.

practical support

- Practice being in a loving state with others—soft, kind, and gentle. Avoid saying things that are likely to create a reaction for them.
- Learn to let go of worrying about what others think of you.
- Learn how to handle conflict well and approach it as an opportunity to develop greater understanding and compassion between both parties.
- Use the following formula as a guide when sharing your feelings with someone in times of conflict:
  - Consciously breathe from you chest or "heart space" to diffuse any tension in your body. Speak from a loving perspective when communicating (you will know when you are in this state as you will be able to feel it in your body).
  - *Respond* by saying how *you* feel rather than criticising or blaming.
  - Share your feelings in a way that they will be heard by using the following guidelines:
    - I feel _____
      (• name the feeling)
    - When _____
      (• describe the situation • stick to ONE incident, or the person will feel overwhelmed • do not use the word YOU, as it can make the other person feel attacked and defensive)
    - Brainstorm an outcome that suits you both.
      _____
      (• consider ideas that would suit you both, be open and flexible in your approach—things may turn out better than you imagine!)

chapter eleven

children are
the light

Children are naturally joyful, shining lights. Their sense of joy and wonder comes from within. The more consciously children are parented the more they are able to retain their state of well-being and happiness.

Children can be a reflection of your internal state. If they are fighting, check to see what *you* are thinking. If you are thinking negative thoughts, change to positive ones without saying anything to them. You may be surprised to find that they stop arguing by themselves. Never underestimate the power of thought! Of course, your children could be fighting because they are tired, hungry, or due to some other influence. However, as a general rule, the calmer, happier, and more present adults are, the happier and calmer the child. Make it your number one priority to provide a safe and happy environment for your child.

The more conscious you are as a parent, the more likely you are to understand how your feelings affect your behaviour towards your child. For example, if you feel happy inside, you are more likely to relate to your child in a happy way. Sometimes you may feel angry, and that is perfectly normal. However, the difference is how conscious you are and the skills you have around your anger. If you are able to recognise that you feel angry and observe it until it passes, you are unlikely to act out the anger in a detrimental way towards your child.

As a parent, being responsible for your happiness is essential. Everyone has their *moments*, however, when something or someone takes you away from feeling happiness, it is important to develop the skills to return to a peaceful place (see chapter 5). Demonstrating this skill to your child, models how to maintain emotional stability when dealing with life's challenges. Do not expect miracles from your child if you are not in a good state yourself. Children are very sensitive to energy. They pick up on your energy constantly and will act out on it, if you are not managing it yourself.

Be mindful of how present you are with your child. Do you get down to their level and really listen to them? Are you aware of the signals of their bodies? Do you link their physical pain to what is going on in their world emotionally? For example, if a child regularly has stomach-aches, it could be a reflection of his or her emotional state.

You can use physical symptoms to understand your child and support them at a deeper level. For example, perhaps they are sad, one of their teachers has left school, but don't have the words to express how they feel. The sad, unexpressed emotion gets trapped in the body as a stomachache. Chatting to them regularly about their concerns helps to keep their emotions flowing. You don't need to solve their problems. Instead offer your support and facilitate them working things out for themselves. With awareness of how the mind and body work together, you will help your child maintain their mind-body connection throughout their life.

Physical symptoms that a child may experience that could relate to the way they are feeling emotionally include:

- Headaches
- Stomachaches
- Skin disorders
- ADHD
- Anxiety
- Depression
- Asthma
- Colds, influenza
- Bed-wetting

It is important to keep the lines of communication open between you and your child. This does not mean you need to know every single detail about their world. Rather, take an interest and be there for them when they need you. This is the concept of *space and support*. Allow them the *space* so they have a sense of freedom to be themselves, while providing *support*, so they know you are always there when they need you.

A child is more likely to come to you and open up if you do not judge them. Validate how they feel (you do not have to agree with their experience), and they will feel unconditionally loved. Of course, boundaries around health and safety are important in caring for their well-being. Other than that, if you have faith and trust your child, they will constantly delight you with how well they know themselves. They know what is right for them and have an innate ability to handle life.

You are born with wings ~ Rumi

Children are intrinsically joyful beings with a strong sense of self. Supporting them in an environment of love is the best gift you can give them. You don't need to *give* them a strong sense of self; they innately possess it. Your job, as a guardian, is to ensure that their sense of self is not interfered with or diminished in any way. Adults are there to:

- Love and accept children as they are
- Keep them safe
- Cater for their physical needs
- Provide space and support for their emotional needs.

Apart from that, all you have to do is enjoy their company and watch them blossom. Recognise, value, and be open to the wisdom of children. I love teaching my children about the world while valuing their innate wisdom. They are constantly evolving me to be a kinder and more compassionate person. I find that we learn from each other.

If your relationship with your child is not peaceful and harmonious, it may be useful to look at the quality of *your* internal world. Is it harmonious and peaceful? Are you happy in your life? Are you demonstrating to your child the behaviours you'd like to see in them, such as kindness, love, and compassion? This does not mean being perfect all the time or expecting your child to be perfect. It is not about setting unrealistic standards, but about being authentic. When mistakes or accidents happen, rather than seeing them as bad or as problems, see them as opportunities to learn and grow. Everyone makes mistakes—as a parent or a child you are likely to do or say things sometimes that you don't mean. Take responsibility for your behaviour and say sorry if necessary and teach your child, by example, how to forgive and say sorry in appropriate situations. This will allow you to maintain loving bonds with each other.

Guilt is an emotion that doesn't serve either parent or child. Short-term guilt may exist to tell you that you are not spending enough time together, for example. If possible, make the appropriate changes to spend more time with your child. Don't hang onto guilt for a prolonged period without changing things, if you can. If you have sorted things out to the best of your ability, stop feeling guilty, knowing that you have made the best choices possible in a given situation. Guilt only weighs you and those around you down, rather than allowing you and your child to enjoy the time you do have together. Forgiveness is the antidote to guilt, including forgiving and setting realistic standards for yourself.

Sometimes big life events take place in children's lives, such as separations, divorces, loss of a home, or a natural disaster. Give yourself the gift of knowing you are dealing with the situation to the best of your ability, while giving your child the best support you can. Kindness and compassion for your child and *yourself* are essential when facing the challenges of life. Reconnect to that loving part of you that knows that you are making the wisest decision possible in your current circumstances. When you feel loving towards yourself, generally you are more likely to deal with your child in a loving way.

With children, a balanced energy flow is important. If parents interact with their child in a controlling way, they are taking their child's energy, which makes them feel weak. If a child runs the home because they are not given boundaries, it results in unempowered parents. A child without boundaries can grow up without a solid sense of self, feeling unsupported and confused. Equal giving and receiving of energy between parent and child is ideal. Both parties then connect and communicate from their hearts. This builds a sustainable child-parent relationship on a solid foundation of love.

If you have had a difficult relationship with your child in the past, it is never too late to develop a wonderful relationship starting from now. This may take time and effort, but can lead to great joy. Genuine heartfelt words, spoken at the right time, can create significant shifts in your relationship quickly. Acknowledge that you may not have behaved as you would have liked in the past and validate how that must have made them feel. Try not to make excuses for your behaviour, but instead focus on them and their feelings. Give them space to talk without interruption if they need it. You are likely to be surprised at how loving and forgiving they may be. Then live up to creating a more loving future for them. Endeavour to be as present as possible as you create a new beginning. Cherish the moments you have together. Show an open loving heart full of humility, and you are likely to be shown the same in return.

Let children be themselves, while you love them as they are and act as guardians of their inner light. Allow their light to shine by having faith and trust that they are whole and perfect as they are, with their unique character, gifts, and talents.

Allow children to shine.

practical support

- Be aware of your attitudes towards your child. Select the ones that support them the best. For example, replace thoughts such as "My child is shy and withdrawn," with, "My child is open and loving." Your attitude reinforces how a child sees themself and how they will be in the world.
- Be present when you are with your child.
- Get down to their level, look into their eyes, and listen with your heart.
- Allow time and space for them to express their feelings.
- Accept *all* their feelings without judgement.
- Respect their opinions and ideas *even if they differ from yours.*
- Recognise and value that you are constantly learning from each other.
- Set clear boundaries around health, safety, and respect for themselves and others.
- Teach them to be flexible and accepting of situations as they arise (chances are they will be teaching *you* to be spontaneous).
- Allow imperfection as normal for both of you.
- View mistakes as learning experiences.
- Provide a non-pressurized environment, filling their world with things and activities that they love.
- If you are struggling with problems in bringing up your child, such as toddler tantrums or teenage rebellion, it can be helpful to take an age-appropriate course, read a book, or seek professional help. New information can help you solve the issue in a loving way before it turns into a big issue that is more difficult to deal with. Support yourself when necessary, however, never let another "expert" override your internal wisdom. Make decisions based on your intuition.
- *Cherish* your beautiful children.

chapter twelve

enlightened
business

business can be a wonderful source of happiness. It can be a place of great fulfilment and connection as people come together to share ideas, create, and evolve in the workplace.

Business can be an opportunity to build something from nothing. Business adds value to the economy and forms communities. This can create dynamic, innovative places for people to interact and grow. Business has the power to affect positive, social change, and make a difference to the general mood of society.

Business is the lifeblood of the community. When business is doing well, the economy is buoyant, open, and expansive. This has a flow on effect in the lives of individuals as seen in Table 3. However, when business is not doing well, the economic and individual mood is usually more contracted and negative.

Table 3: The effect of the economy on individuals

Economic Recession	Economic Expansion
• Contracted state	• Open and expansive
• Require strong leadership	• Able to self-direct
• More fearful	• Willing to take risks
• More inclined to gossip	• Less likely to gossip
• Less creative	• Innovative
• Less interactive	• Interactive
• Less engaged	• Engaged
• Discontented	• Happy
• More disconnected	• Connected
• Focused on survival rather than growth	• Focused on achieving personal and business goals

The challenge for business is to remain in an open and expanded state *even when times are difficult.* A business, during difficult economic times, may need to contract for a period of time while it regroups and develops a plan of action. Ideally, it will then move forward, *responding* rather than *reacting* to circumstances.

Difficult economic times can give business the opportunity be more effective and efficient—to bring a fresh and new perspective to the way things are done. Economic change can also give people the opportunity to start new careers that are more in line with their true purpose (see chapter 8).

Long-term success and happiness in life, including your career, depends on your personal qualities. Your personal qualities, such as courage, resilience, and awareness, allow you to survive and handle situations as they arise. This ultimately gives you *freedom from* mental entrapment. There is truth in the saying: *it is not the problem but the way that you handle it that makes the difference.*

Everyone possesses courage and resilience. When you are doing work you love, it is usually easier to cope with difficult times, as your passion helps you to endure any challenges. Sometimes you will need to tap into your courage and resilience on the journey toward doing the work that you love. For example, it takes courage to change careers in order to do what it is you really want to do. It takes resilience to complete the long hours of study required to become a doctor or a lawyer, for example.

The more engaged you are in your career, the more enjoyable you will find it. This does not necessarily mean working long hours; but is about being present and focused while you are at work.

Work flow cycle

Business is often associated with stress, pressure, and a huge emphasis on making money. Of course, a business needs to be financially secure to survive. Usually the more profitable a business the better benefits and wages it is able to offer its employees. The more profitable ideally, everybody is able to flourish. However, it is possible to sacrifice a lot in terms of your personal life, happiness, and health to make money. Business doesn't have to be like this, but in many cases it is the path that is taken.

Personal compromise can occur due to the thought that when you have lots of money, you will *then* be happy. Money does give choices, which is definitely a component of happiness. However, money will never, ever *substitute* for inner contentment. Being happy and enjoying your journey is the important thing. Inner peace and material success can co-exist.

It is possible for business to be fun, light, positive, happy, *and* financially successful. *It is possible to have it all.* While there may be challenging times, business does not have to be a struggle on a long-term basis. People generally spend a relatively large proportion of their life working. Work can be a fun and wonderful experience. Work is an amazing opportunity for people to grow, expand awareness, and develop personal qualities.

As mentioned previously, one of the keys to happiness, is to engage in work that you love and is meaningful to you. From this happy, joyful place you are more likely to advance and be promoted than if you are struggling away in some job that you hate.

If businesses were led and supported by people who loved what they were doing, the world would be entirely different. The flow-on effect would be enormous. No one would need to come home regularly in a bad mood or have to have a drink to recover from their day at work.

Generally the leader determines the mood or the culture of a business. If the leader has clear purpose, loves what they do, has good communication, conflict resolution, and business skills, the energy of the business is more likely to be positive and sustainable. Good leaders have the ability to develop new skills when challenges arise, enabling them to work through difficulties and stabilise the business.

When a leader is very clear in his or her purpose, that clarity usually reflects in a clear company vision, mission, and goals. This makes it easier to employ the right people for the company and for people to know if it is the right company for them.

Over the past few decades, there has been a lot of talk and movement toward collaborative business. However, in many cases this model is a concept, rather than a reality. Leaders often have power over employees and suppliers for there own benefit rather than everyone working together to achieve common goals and objectives. Alternatively, many employees have power over their employers, doing their job grudgingly, but taking their pay anyway.

How congruent you are as a person is important when it comes to integrity in business. For instance, if you treat your family well and then go to work and retrench someone without dignity—having them marched to the door by security—there is a divide in the way you do things. Sometimes people have to be retrenched, but it is possible to do this with compassion and kindness.

Alternatively, if you believe you live your life with integrity and expect people to treat you honestly and then go to work and think it's okay to steal even a few pens from your employer, there is incongruence in your behaviour. When you act with integrity, whether at home or work, it helps to build the business world on a solid foundation.

This is a time for business to evolve from adolescence to adulthood in terms of people taking responsibility and giving work their best. If you are a leader or manager, see it as a privilege and an honour to engage with the hearts and minds of other human beings.

If you have made a decision to be in paid employment, you will feel better if you do work you love. It is then easy to do a great job. If you are doing something as a stepping stone to get to the work you really want to do, make the most of it while you are there. It makes you and everyone around you feel better.

Business helps to shape the world and make dreams come true. When business comes from a place of passion and general love of products and services, rather than from being driven to meet material needs or a lack of self-worth, it is more enjoyable and sustainable in the longer term.

It is possible to have it all.

practical support

- Treat everybody with the same respect: family, clients, work colleagues, employees, and suppliers.
- Be congruent and authentic in all levels of business.
- Ensure that you are engaged in or on the path to work that you love (see chapter 8).
- Ensure that company and employees' goals are a good fit.
- If you love your work, but feel stressed, improving your skills can help. For example, you may feel under pressure in relation to leadership, interpersonal, or technical skills. Finding a book, course, or mentor can improve your knowledge and increase your confidence.
- Inspire and innovate at all levels, whether you are a leader or team member.

chapter thirteen

embrace
the ego

Your ego develops to keep you safe from threats and dangers that you may experience in life. It aims to protect you by closing you down and creating a hard shell. This shell (also known as a *defence,* or as a friend of mine more lovingly refers to it, a *coping mechanism*), then judges and keeps you separate from others, so that in theory you won't get hurt. This approach, however, does not work in the long term. It is only when you are open, gentle, trusting, accepting, and loving that you develop the ability to connect with the loving source energy that is present in everyone.

Your ego *thinks* it is in control and running the show—yet it is the source of all your pain and suffering. It stops you from listening to your intuition, wisdom, or God. In order to transcend your ego to a place of peace, it needs to be understood with love and accepted as it is. Shining love on your ego helps you to transcend its power.

The energy of your ego can be very influential. It is the part of you that convinces you that you're not good enough, not smart enough, and/or you need to struggle to be worthy of a good life. It convinces you that you need to compete with others, that you are better, worse, richer, poorer, fatter, skinnier. Your ego loves to compare. This comparison keeps you attached to striving and wanting more, to feeling unacceptable as you are, and to generally being trapped by the ego's power!

Your ego is constructed by your mind. It is the sum total of your thoughts, beliefs and attitudes. These thoughts, beliefs and attitudes usually come from what others tell you and what you tell yourself. It is when you go beyond these constructs that you are able to begin to operate from a state of love also known as *presence.* As your ego (also known as mind), is constructed by what you take on from the external world, it is also possible to deconstruct the ego, by perceiving the external world differently. This is done by understanding your internal world—your thoughts, feelings, physical body and your reactions, so that you can make choices around these areas. By learning to view your inner world with love, particularly the parts that are hurting or you find difficult to face, you can begin to *transform your life to one of peace and happiness.*

The ego is fuelled by *duality*. Duality is a concept from the wisdom of ancient India and refers to the opposing nature of things: pleasure and pain, right and wrong, joy and grief, for example. Duality engages you in a life constantly dancing between opposite forces, such as feeling happy and sad. When you feel happy, you feel good, and when you feel sad, you usually strive to make yourself feel happy again. The dance between opposing forces usually involves struggle and/or pain. The ego likes struggle, as this is what keeps it alive. It convinces us that when we are sad, that is bad and we need to do whatever it takes to get us back on track to feeling happy again. The ego keeps us busy and generally makes us work hard to meet its demands.

Maya is an Indian term that refers to the dualistic or oppositional forces of human experience as an *illusion*. This philosophy involves the belief that you are separate from God or love (they are exactly the same thing), rather than at one with God. *It is this separation from love that is the source of all our pain and misery.* The ego would have you believe that you are not the creation but the creator, and that keeps you separate from who you really are, which is love. This idea of separation keeps you entrapped in the illusion of Maya.

Transcending pain and suffering involves the reconnection to your source, which is love. You are a creation of God and are in fact love (or God)—not separate. When you feel connected to your source, you automatically feel in a natural state of love and happiness. For example, when I feel unhappy or uneasy, or am having a reaction to something, I know I need to give myself some space, to return to my natural state of love. I calm my mind by focussing on my breath and becoming present by focussing on my footsteps or what is going on around me, for example. If I am hurting inside, I shine my love on it (without wanting a quick fix from somewhere else to ease the pain) until I feel comforted and better. This is helpful in transcending whatever pain and suffering my mind is creating. When I have calmed myself and am in my natural loving state, my wisdom guides me, and I am able to see the situation with a new loving perspective that does not cause me pain. When my decisions are based on love, I know they are right for me.

To transcend suffering, pain, and the illusion of Maya, it is also helpful to accept situations as they are. When you go beyond judgement about whether a situation is good or bad, right or wrong, you are able to view things from a more relaxed, objective, state. When you diffuse the stress around a situation, often created by judgement, you are more likely to connect to your internal wisdom. That is why you are able to remember where you put the keys once you stop looking for them; or why you remember what you wanted to say once you stop trying hard to remember what it was!

If you are struggling, stressed, or in pain, your ego is firmly in charge. If you feel loving towards yourself and others, you know you are connected to who you really are, and that is love. For example, your day could be going well and you feel happy and content. You get a phone call from someone who says something that completely takes you away from your peace. Six hours later you could still be obsessing and stressing about that telephone call, blaming the person who called you for ruining your day! The ego keeps you trapped in your pain and loves to create drama around any possible situation.

However, if you were to transcend illusions of Maya, you would acknowledge that you are in emotional pain after the telephone conversation and firmly in the grip of the ego. Recognise that pain is a result of the ego and not who you are. Calm your mind in the best way for you—focus on the beauty of nature, your breath, be really present. If you are hurting because you've had a reaction during that phone call, shine love on it. Another way to look at it is to hand the issue over to God or love, which will intuitively guide you back to your peace. Trust, listen, and take *action* on what your intuition is telling you. You will know your intuition is talking to you because it will feel right! Your intuition may be telling you to make difficult changes or speak your truth. This may be uncomfortable in the short term, but will definitely benefit your overall sense of well-being and happiness.

It can also be helpful to recognise that nobody else can make you feel—your feelings are *your* feelings. Once you take full responsibility for your feelings, your ego is no longer in control. The ego loves chaos, controversy, control, conflict, and particularly blame! It wants you to believe that everyone else is at fault—and that you are right and others are wrong. Ultimately, this creates separation and cuts you off from your true source of power, which is your loving self.

When you live your life according to the principle that it is more important to be kind (love) than right (ego), the ego is no longer running your life.

> *By passion for the "pairs of opposites".*
> *By those twain snares of Like and Dislike, Prince!*
> *All creatures live bewildered, save some few*
> *Who, quit of sins, holy in act, informed,*
> *Freed from the "opposites," and fixed in faith,*
> *Cleave unto me*
> (Bhagavadgita, 1993, 38)

When you recognise and shine love on the ego, you will then begin to transcend mental suffering. When you no longer choose to judge the ego, you can begin to dissolve its power and operate your life from a loving foundation. If you *oppose* the ego, you maintain its power. This is in accordance to Newton's third law of motion: *Every action has an equal and opposite reaction.* When you *accept* the ego, you are able to integrate it into your psyche and feel more peaceful as you have diffused the internal battle. The ego was established to keep you safe; however, it operates from a basis of fear rather than love. You can make a choice to embrace the ego, transcend it, and operate from love rather than being driven by fear.

In conflict it can be helpful to forgive the person who triggered the feelings of unhappiness within you. Simultaneously forgive yourself for thinking the ego was in control and that either one of you were anything other than an expression of love.

When ego is displayed at its worst, in the cases of war, violence, and greed, for example, it is tempting to fight back with ego. However, if we are to evolve and create a new world of peace and harmony—love is always the way to overcome ego. Jesus is a shining example of someone who was able to rise above ego and forgive those who caused him so much pain and suffering. Pope John Paul II did the same thing by forgiving Mehmet Ali Ağca, who had attempted to assassinate him on May 13, 1981. Following his attempted assassination, in which four bullets hit him and left him critically wounded, Pope John Paul II asked people to "pray for my brother (Ağca), whom I have sincerely forgiven." When you are in a loving state, you are less likely to feel the need to attack and defend, as you feel peaceful within yourself.

If you are loving and compassionate on a daily basis, our world will evolve to one of love and compassion. As it is within, so it is without. *There is no force more powerful than love.* Your most powerful way of being is always love. The difference in power between a loving thought ($10^{-35 \text{million}}$ microwatts) and a fearful thought (between $10^{-800 \text{million}}$ microwatts to $10^{-750 \text{ million}}$ microwatts) is so enormous as to be beyond the capacity of the human imagination to easily comprehend. Even a few loving thoughts during the course of the day more than counterbalance all of our negative thoughts (Hawkins, 1995, 235).

It can be humbling and empowering to recognise that faults perceived in others are often aspects of yourself that have come up for healing. Once you own what you see, as *your* experience that it is trying to teach you something about yourself, you can begin to transcend the ego. For example, you may observe that your child is constantly having tantrums. This may really annoy you; indicating you have an emotional charge around it. If so, take the attention off your child for the moment. Ask yourself: "When I don't get my way, do I have an adult version of a tantrum?" If so, this honesty, and awareness, can start to change things for you and your child. You can begin to transcend the ego and the grip of its power. It may be helpful for you and your child to learn alternative ways of communicating other than having a tantrum. For example, learn to calm yourself down and then say what is true for you in a loving way.

Significant transformation is possible when ego is recognised at the following three levels:

1. **Personally.** Acceptance is a sign that your ego is loosing its power. When you are taken away from your peace, lovingly recognise it as your ego at work. For example, if you find yourself angry, in pain, or feel guilty, lovingly recognise that is not who you are, but instead your ego at work. Focus

on your breath; take your mind off the problem and focus on the present. Hand the problem over to your loving self, your intuition, or God (however you choose to see it); that will guide you back to peace.

Once you accept the duality within yourself (good feelings such as happiness and painful feelings such as anger), you transcend labelling certain parts of yourself as wrong or right. This is an integral part of loving yourself just as you are. This step is essential in accepting and loving others as they are. You cannot transcend your pain by pretending it does not exist. Pain can be used as alchemy to transcend to your natural loving state. By accepting pain rather than resisting it and looking to solutions when you feel loving rather than reacting and acting out in fear, you are evolving to a more loving and peaceful way of being.

2. **Interpersonally.** When you accept others as they are, you create loving relationships, rather than ones based on fear and judgement. When you see faults in others, it is a sign you are seeing them from the perspective of the ego. When your ego is not involved, you see others as the loving individuals they are. You can learn to relate to people beyond judgement and defence. In conflict it is possible to rise above blame and seeing problems as the other person's fault. Learning new skills to appreciate and respect differences builds stronger, more loving and interesting relationships. It was only after I separated from my husband that I learned to go beyond the negative, destructive thoughts of the ego and appreciate him for the love that he is. Everyone experiences the world in an individual way, and it is respectful to let others experience the world their way.

Ego would have you think that you are right and that others who think like you are right. When you view people through the eyes of love, you are genuinely interested and respect their unique perspective. You become more open. When you view the world in this way, people are more comfortable to be themselves around you, as they do not fear judgement. It is difficult for people to grow and transcend behaviours while they are being judged and criticised. Even a hardened criminal who is shown deep love and respect (something they may never have experienced in their entire life) has the potential for transformation. As we learn to relate to each other in a loving way we can transcend the energy of the ego.

3. **Globally.** A major shift will occur on our planet when love replaces the controlling nature of the ego. When we accept that the ego has been instrumental in causing all violence, wars, and poverty, we will make positive, lasting changes toward a more loving world. Judgement, striving to win at the expense of others, racial, cultural, and religious differences, have all been major sources of suffering. When we stop seeing challenging situations as something *out there,* beyond our control, we can effect change. When we collectively take responsibility for the state of the world as it is, we can transcend the energy of the ego. We can be loving individuals, engaged in loving relationships that in turn will have a flow-on effect in creating a world of peace.

When you operate from love, you create loving relationships, communities, and nations. When people embody love, it will become the predominant energy on our planet, and our world will transform to one of peace, love, and harmony.

Transform your life to one of peace and happiness.

practical support

- Be aware that ongoing pain and suffering can be the result of your ego. Not in times of natural grief, but more in terms of day-to-day occurrences of life. Develop an awareness of what the pain is related to. Hand this problem to love or God by visualisation and/or intent. Answers will come to you regarding the appropriate course of action from your intuition.

- Regularly ask yourself: "Are your choices being determined by ego or love?" If you hear the voice of ego in your mind (*should* voice, guided by fear), lovingly accept this and choose to change your thoughts to loving ones that allow you to feel good.

- Make *happiness* the goal of your choices.

chapter fourteen

embody love

■ t is easy to spend your whole life looking for love, yet you are
love. *You are love.* Pure, divine, love. When you recognise
this and start to live your life as a loving expression, you will
be true to yourself. When you become free from the grip of the
mind and begin to operate from your *heart space*, your whole life
will begin to change. When you express love—this is what will
be reflected back to you.

You may have to endure challenging situations; however,
learning to deal with them lovingly is the best possible way. When
challenges are met with fear, it can prolong or escalate the issue,
fuelled by destructive thoughts. It is possible to transcend the
mind so that you feel in control, rather than being controlled by
the pain your mind can create. Pain is an illusion of the mind.
Your natural state is love. You may find yourself taken away from
this state from time to time. With awareness, you can develop the
skills to return to your loving self when this happens.

If you perceive others as anything other than love, chances are
you are not seeing yourself from a loving viewpoint. When you are
triggered or find yourself judging someone, ask yourself, "What
is it that I am judging in myself?" Life is like a mirror, reflecting
back to you, your internal world. When you lovingly forgive
someone for the fault you perceive in him or her, simultaneously
forgive yourself for the fault you see in yourself. Forgiveness
helps you to return to your natural loving state. *All faults are an
illusion.* They are your ego's trick to create judgement and keep
you separate from freedom and love.

Your ego will tell you that being confused, in pain, stressed,
anxious, depressed, struggling and needing more is just part of
life. Your perception of the world around you reflects how you feel
internally. When you use the messages life gives you as a gift, by
taking full, *loving* responsibility for your reactions, you have the
opportunity to grow and, over time, come to experience and act
from your natural state of love.

In Chinese medicine the heart is seen as the emperor of the
body, emotionally and physically. Physically without a heart you
cannot survive. Emotionally, if your heart is hurting, it can block
you from experiencing the natural joy that is inherent in life.

If someone is hurting at a deep level, it is possible that they
are protecting their heart with a defensive layer of anger. This is

to stop people getting too close and possibly hurting them again. Underneath anger there is usually a layer of sadness, then a layer of hurt and underlying everything there is *always* love. Everything always comes back to love, as *love is at the core of your being.*

The layers of defence

Rather than denying anger, you can move towards your natural loving state, by learning how to own and feel it a little bit at a time. It is possible that it has served as a defence mechanism or as a coping mechanism to date. Becoming aware of and accepting your defence mechanisms over time enables you to create new loving behaviours. It is possible to return to feeling deeply peaceful and happy. Ultimately the aim is to create the life that you want rather than one driven by defences.

To make peace with your defences:

1. Feel and observe anger, rather than suppressing it with alcohol, drugs, or reacting to it in ways that could hurt others. This could be through meditation, journaling angry feelings, or doing physical sport. Look at your anger from a compassionate, kind viewpoint—you could even visualise giving it a hug!

2. Sadness often surfaces once you have processed your anger. Observe it, without judgement. You may feel like crying which can make you feel better as it releases pressure that has been used to hold back unresolved sadness.

3. Underneath sadness is often hurt. You may actually feel physical pain in your heart. If so observing the pain with love helps to heal and open your heart. The following is a guide on how to do this:

    – *Sit in a comfortable meditation position.*
    – *Observe any emotional pain in your body without reaction or judgement.*
    – *Focus on your breath and on creating a sense of space around the pain. Your breath will begin to re-oxygenate your body, restore your sense of calm and revitalise the way you feel. It will begin to connect you to your natural loving state. This could take at least ten minutes depending on how you are feeling and then the body will usually relax. When you are relaxed it is easier to focus on your breath. Stay with the process despite any resistance. Do not resist the resistance! Just accept and observe any resistance, allowing it to flow, connecting you to your natural state of love.*
    – *See the breath as love flowing in and out of your body, healing and nurturing.*

At this point, it is also useful to ask: "What story (thoughts) have I been telling myself around my anger, sadness and hurt?" For example, the story could be because my father left me when I was young resulting in the unconscious belief that *I am unlovable.* Usually the story that you have been telling yourself creates the feelings. If the feeling has come up for healing by way of reactive anger, it is usually time to observe the anger and underlying sadness, hurt, and the resulting story and let them go. *To create peace: accept and then let go of the story that has been creating mental pain, reflected in your hurting heart.* Perhaps you have not been loved exactly as you would have liked; however, now as an adult you can nurture and love yourself anytime and anywhere. Instead of pain, choose forgiveness, acceptance, and love to facilitate true healing.

Pain is a defence or a layer in your body. It is an illusion that is not real. To move through it you must acknowledge it and embrace it. Your defences are the best way you knew until now, but through awareness it is possible to choose a more peaceful and happy way of being. Your breath will love, heal and nurture any emotional pain you may be experiencing. The breath—unlike your defences—is real, strong, safe, secure and ever present. It is a physical reminder of who you really are! *The breath connects you back to your loving nature and is what connects us to each other.* Our breath reminds us that we are not alone but are always supported by loving energy. We just have to choose to let it in! Breath deeply, regularly and consciously and you will!

Meditating for twenty minutes per day connects you to your loving self. By focusing on love, it enables you to more easily bring loving action into the rest of your life.

The experience of turning pain into love is alchemy, creating peace and joy. For example, you will find after healing your heart with love, you are less likely to put yourself in situations that cause you suffering. As you value and respect yourself you are more likely to speak your truth and get your needs met. You will find yourself focussing on activities and spending time with people you love. You are more likely to bring joy to places there has been no joy.

Learn to understand and observe the energy of your heart. Does it feel small and closed or is it open and expansive? Does it feel cold or warm? Can you feel your heart at all? If your heart feels cold, small or closed, consciously begin to open it a little at a time. Give love in terms of trusting and allowing people to become close to you. Receive love by accepting compliments, hugs and warm words, for example. This may feel uncomfortable at first because you are learning a new way of being. However with practice, giving and receiving love will feel natural.

If others are reactive and angry, let them have their experience, and love them as they are. Chances are that if you are seeing them as reactive and angry, you have not healed these aspects within yourself. *Love is always the answer.* Consciously choose a loving perspective and don't allow yourself to feel that you need to attack or feel defensive. When operating from love or truth, there is no need to defend or attack. The Foundation for Inner Peace has written:

> *Let no defences but your present trust direct the future, and this life becomes a meaningful encounter with the truth that only your defences would conceal. Without defences, you become a light, which Heaven gratefully acknowledges to be its own. And it will lead you on in ways appointed for your happiness according to the ancient plan, begun when time was born.* (A Course in Miracles, 1975, 248)

You want to feel love because you are love—innately your soul is calling you home. You just have to become attuned to the signs. Attempts to fill the emptiness inside you by trying to connect to love externally ultimately lead to dissatisfaction and disappointment. True love, self-worth, and connection come from within. Then all the love reflected back to you is just a bonus to the love that you already are.

The world we have created externally is a collective reflection of our internal world. As each individual truly *feels* that they are divine love—not just understanding it as an intellectual concept—they will embody love and *know* they are home.

You want to feel love because you are love.

practical support

- Process anger, sadness and hurt, while meditating or through awareness of your feelings:
  - Acknowledge and observe your anger in a non-judgemental way without reacting to it or acting upon it.
  - Once the anger has passed, you may feel sad. Acknowledge and observe the feeling. Crying can help you feel better as it releases any unresolved emotions.
  - Underneath sadness is usually hurt. Nurture hurt with your own love using the following meditation:
    - *Observe any pain in your body without reaction or judgement.*
    - *Focus on your breath and creating a sense of space around the pain. Allow at least ten minutes for your body to relax. Accept and observe any resistance allowing it to flow and allowing you to go deeper within and connect to your natural state of love.*
    - *See the breath as love flowing in and out of your body, healing and nurturing*
- If you perceive fault in yourself or others, remind yourself that all faults are an illusion. *The truth is love.*
- *Consciously choose love.* Endeavor to make every action loving—even when those around you are not. See the best in yourself and others. If you find yourself reacting, learn the lesson, and return to your state of peace.
- *Consciously give love.* Think, speak, and act lovingly. Trust people and allow them to become close to you. Give compliments, kind deeds and hugs freely!

- *Consciously receive love.* Be open to people loving the beautiful person that you are. Accept compliments, hugs, and kind deeds with gratitude. Sounds easy, but really let them into *your heart.*
- Fill your life with joy. Do things that you love, for example, a crossword, singing, dancing, or painting.
- Notice the joy in the little things. A smile, watching children walk to school, the sunshine on the trees, a kind word between people. *Joy is everywhere once you tune into it.*

chapter fifteen

bliss exposed

lowing with life, leads to bliss. Living in an aware way, from a state of love and presence is integral to this process. Accepting yourself and others as they are, while being open to new possibilities creates a sense of peace and harmony.

When you go beyond thought, beyond ego, you will find this peaceful, yet dynamic, state. You feel energetic, complete, and absorbed in the moment. You are not obsessing about the past or worrying about the future. You may have challenging times; however, you are able to use your skills to centre yourself back to your loving self. This enables you to make kind and benevolent decisions, rather than those based on fear.

Living from a state of loving awareness rather than being controlled by the mind, allows you to be in tune with the flow of life. Life unfolds in a more synchronistic, effortless way. Rather than being out of step with life you are instead dancing in tune. When you live from awareness, you feel connected to everything around you. *This state does not require any external circumstances to change.* It requires only that you shift your perception to a place beyond thought, negativity, fear and rest in peace and harmony. Here you will find yourself connected to your intuition, which safely guides you on your journey through life.

When you live your life with awareness, it is like being connected to a dynamic, all-knowing intelligence field that has the answers to everything. It is the wisdom that you find when you go beyond thought and listen.

If you become aware of yourself thinking negative or obsessive thoughts, this is a valuable opportunity to practice developing your awareness. Consciously stop thinking thoughts! Shift your focus from your head to your body. Let your attention rest in your body and relax. When you consciously shift awareness in this way, it feels good because you are releasing the tension and stress in your head that results from over-thinking. With an empty mind there is room to experience the peace and love that is inherently within you. When you are stressed it masks your inner peace. Practice taking a walk in nature, without being lost in your thoughts. Consciously focus on your surroundings—your footsteps, the way the light touches the trees, the sound of the birds singing, and so on. This shift in perception allows you to be fully present and to feel the joy of the moment—it allows you to experience the presence that exists beyond the mind.

The following table will give you clues to indicate when you are being controlled by your mind (or ego) and when you are in your natural state of presence.

Table 4: Characteristics of Mind and Presence

Mind	Presence
• Stress	• Trusts
• Disharmony	• Harmonious
• Division	• Connection
• Narrow focus	• Open
• Limits	• Creates
• Imperfection	• Perfection
• Not enough	• Complete as is
• Hard	• Gentle
• Driving	• Flowing
• Lack	• Abundance
• Heavy	• Light, playful
• Criticizes	• Appreciates
• Judges	• Accepts

When you are being controlled by your mind consciously use this awareness to create a state of peace within yourself. For example, stop criticizing, obsessing or worrying about money—or whatever form of illusion the mind is partaking in—and return to being focussed on the present moment. As your mind loses its grip on you, you will find your life opening up in a new, loving way.

Unawareness leads to doing the same thing again, even if it makes you unhappy. Awareness of your thoughts, feelings, body, reactions, and resulting behaviours enables you to make changes if you desire. That is why awareness is the ultimate freedom. The freedom to make choices and live the life you want rather than being driven by unconscious behavioural patterns that do not serve you. Consciously look at any emotional pain within you with love. Love dissolves pain and when your heart opens up it feels blissful. You can spend a lifetime looking for bliss *out there* while it has been inside you the whole time!

Self-acceptance is an important step on the journey to bliss. When you don't accept yourself as you are, you falsely believe you are not good enough or that you are something other than love.

These beliefs separate you from your true divine, loving nature; they overshadow the love that you are. You are already perfect. The journey to yourself is about changing your perception so that you *feel* the goodness within you, rather than just understanding it as an intellectual concept.

My journey has taught me that I am still acceptable and of value regardless of my financial position. When my relationships and the world changes around me, I am still valuable. At my core I know that I am always acceptable and loveable, regardless of external circumstances. I know that when I am challenged, I can reach inside myself to access the inner strength and state of peace that will guide me through any situation.

I have learned that when I truly accept myself (rather than thinking something is wrong with me), I feel lighter, happier, and more blissful. Can you ever remember having a conversation with someone and they really seemed to *get* you? They seemed to be on your wavelength, and you felt understood. When you begin to *get* yourself—you learn to appreciate yourself regardless of external circumstances. You understand you have a light and a shadow side. To accept both your light and shadow helps you to be more loving towards yourself. From this place of acceptance you can then develop skills to change your behaviours if you want to.

Sometimes you may not know the answers to questions, feel confused, and as though your life is in chaos. Accepting that you don't know everything right now and having faith that the answer will come at the right time—allows you to flow with life rather than push against it. Accepting that you are grieving, sad, or angry helps you to stay in tune with your feelings and lets them flow and be processed in a natural way. Observing the feeling with love, rather than letting the feeling control you, is the key to emotional stability.

You don't need to try hard or work hard on yourself; that just creates unnecessary pressure and is exhausting. When things happen in your life, when you accept the situation (and this will be in your timeframe), it helps you to process things naturally. When you resist or push against what is happening, that resistance maintains the stuck energy around it. When I sold my home, it took years for me to truly accept my situation. I fought against it, not validating how sad I really felt. Accepting how I was feeling would have helped me to move through that situation in a way that did not prolong or draw out the pain.

Acceptance allows you to relax and tune in to the appropriate course of action for you. When you relax, it is easier to listen to yourself with love and find the right path. Even if you later find that you are off course, you can always adjust and modify your actions until it feels right for you. There are no mistakes, only learnings.

Acceptance helps you to transcend and move through circumstances. For example, accepting that you have an ego helps you to make choices around it. When you embrace the ego, you transcend it, allowing you to feel more peaceful and loving. If you do not accept that you have an ego (denial) or fight against it, it maintains its power. What you resist persists! However, when you accept the ego as part of your emotional development, you diffuse its power and the tension it creates. You are then free to develop a new level of emotional stability. When the ego tries to influence you with fearful thoughts, with awareness, you can choose loving ones instead.

You feel more fulfilled when you accept yourself just as you are. Rather than striving to be good, acceptance allows you to experience the natural goodness of yourself and others. Accepting the duality of life, your ego and loving side, your shadow and light, your pleasure and pain, and your judgement and non-judgement, helps you to relax. When you relax, you automatically do things from choice rather than from feeling driven and pushed. When you relax, you are able to access your intuition and wisdom.

When you don't accept yourself as you are, you can be left feeling that you are wrong or not good enough in some way. My journey taught me it is exhausting trying to *fix* others and myself, and believe me I've tried! Trying to fix yourself or someone else comes from a more judgemental view, as something is seen to be wrong in the first place. However, it is possible to change your *perspective, to see yourself and others through the eyes of love.*

You will know what divine love is when you begin to feel your oneness with every human being, not before. (Yogananda, 1944, 19)

When you see a fault or judge another, you are really seeing a fault or judging yourself in some way—as we are as one. *There are no others.* The perception of faults in others reminds us of our fragmentation from God, from love, from who we really are. They are a gift, a reminder to guide us back on our journey to wholeness. By shining love on any perceived faults with loving acceptance, you will return to your natural loving state. Without resistance towards yourself or others, there is only FLOW. No pressure, just love, peace, joy and BLISS!

There are no others.

practical support

- Write a long list of all your good points: the things you love about yourself. Things that you may see as weaknesses can often be turned into strengths if you develop a new perspective. For example, for much of my life, I felt I was cursed with being "too sensitive." However, over time I have come to appreciate my gift of sensitivity. Sensitivity allows me to be in tune with what is going on around me.

- Constantly direct your awareness to what you are thinking. If you find you are thinking stressful and negative thoughts, *great*! This is an opportunity to practice shifting to a loving state of awareness. Follow these steps:

  - Consciously stop thinking; shift your awareness from your head to your body. For example, focus on your hands, or the sensation of your feet touching the ground, or try to listen to your heart beating. Consciously shifting awareness from your head to your body feels good, as you release tension and stress created by over thinking.

  - Practice emptying your mind of thoughts anytime, anywhere, and connect to your awareness. This will allow space for peace and love to fill the void of a clear mind.

- Accept life as it is. Do not resist or push against it as this generally creates pain. Think "so be it" or "let it be" to maintain your own sense of well being and happiness. For eternal peace remember, *there are no others*.

chapter sixteen

afterword

bliss every day is available to anyone who wants to transform his or her life to one of peace and happiness. Creating a blissful life is not about competition and striving to be the best at the expense of others. If it were, we would be creating more of the same: a world that in many cases is driven by ego. To evolve we need a complete paradigm shift from the world that we have created.

Paradigm shift is a term popularised by the philosopher and scientist Thomas Kuhn. It refers to people seeing a situation in an entirely new way. Kuhn's work shows how almost every significant breakthrough in the field of science is first a break with tradition, with old ways of thinking, with old paradigms.

The paradigm shift this book refers to is the shift from a world driven by fear to a world founded on love.

It is possible to constantly strive for more and think that happiness exists in the future when goals are achieved. Alternatively happiness can be experienced based on deep inner fulfilment and the loving relationship you have with yourself. This love radiates outwards and is expressed in deep and meaningful relationships. Great joy can be experienced in the expression of skills and talents. Peace and happiness are then more likely to abound on the planet because this is what mankind experiences within. Like little mini-generators, people contribute loving energy to the planet. Love rather than fear will bind our world together.

Positive change is entirely possible. When we accept the world as it is, rather than pushing against it creating more pain and resistance, it paves the way for change. From acceptance, we relax and tap into our awareness that is our innate wisdom. Collectively we are the creators of our future. With awareness we can create the world we desire rather than creating a world that is sometimes based on unconscious behaviours. What we believe becomes our reality. As with other major world movements, such as the women's movement and freedom from slavery, not every single person has to believe that peace on the planet is possible before it becomes a reality.

Change generally begins with 10–15 percent of the population being passionately committed to the change (Adams, 1988, 7–10). When 25–30 percent of the population is consistently supportive of the idea, demonstrated by talking about it, modelling it, and taking action, with persistence despite all obstacles, change is inevitable (Adams, 2003, 6).

If enough of us believe and take action towards creating a world based on love rather than fear, transformation will begin to occur. Loving energy is so powerful that it has the ability to turn our planet into one of beauty and peace. With our world facing much fear, due to impending financial readjustment and issues of world peace, we are being called to action now.

This shift is taking place at the level of the mind. It is a mental shift, as it is from our minds that we collectively create our world. *This new movement is about freedom from mental entrapment.* It is about creating a new way of being, where the mind is free from mental suffering and is instead peaceful.

While violence, fear, greed, hatred, poverty, famine, and hardship currently exist, it is also possible that collectively we can make a difference. To think that you have to single-handedly change the larger, more difficult issues in the world could be overwhelming. However, you *can* commit to changing things in your life for the better, without judging yourself or others in the process. This evolution is not about asking anyone to be perfect but to accept the inherent perfection that is already within. It is about being authentic, accepting, kind, and loving.

By accepting yourself and others, you can begin to relax. You can start to create an authentic, meaningful life, by doing the things that make you really happy. When you connect to your internal happiness system or God, you are able to connect to others in meaningful ways. Through our connection, unity, and love, together we will create the world of peace that we long for.

The second coming of Christ is not about following a particular person or guru, but is about relating to the love of God within all of us. It is not about searching and grasping to find this love externally. The second coming of Christ is that God lives within our hearts. It is possible to live life from loving awareness rather than fear, on a daily basis. When we are able live from awareness, make conscious choices, and express the love that is within us, we will embody God as the human race. This way of being is available to everyone.

The loving nature of mankind is our future. There is no particular person who is the Guru. The Guru lives within us all. *Collectively we are God—we are love.*

Collectively we are God—we are love.

about the author

deborah Fairfull lives in Sydney, Australia, with her family and has been both a student and teacher of psychology and philosophy for over twenty years. She is renowned for inspiring others to achieve unimagined levels of success, happiness, and contentment.

Fairfull's passion and commitment shines through in everything she does. She remains a true leader of our time and continues to change the lives of those she comes in contact with, both now and into the future.

As a former winner of the Australian Capital Territory (ACT) Business Woman of the Year Award, the ACT Chief Minister's Award for Innovation, and the founder of award winning businesses Brave Design Group and Eatsmart Food, Deborah Fairfull enjoys continued success as an industry spokesperson and author.

Fairfull is committed to the ongoing improvement of the world we live in. Her simple, succinct, and practical approach to raising the awareness of individuals allows them connect to true peace and happiness. Fairfull is driven by the capacity to synchronize mind, body, and spirit, and she firmly believes that people have unlimited abilities to heal, change, and grow if they choose to do so.

Along with being a skillful businesswoman and enthusiastic kinesiologist, speaker, and author, Deborah is also a devoted mother. Her three young children are the greatest source of inspiration in her life, and she is passionate about raising children in a positive and conscious way.

Deborah studied design at Charles Stuart University, human resources at the Australian College of Applied Psychology, counseling and psychotherapy at Jansen Newman Institute, and kinesiology at the College of Complementary Medicine. She has been a student of yoga for twenty years.

bibliography

Adams, J. D. Building critical mass for change. *OD Practitioner* 20(2), 1988.

Adams, J. D. Successful Change: paying attention to the intangibles. *OD Practitioner* 35(4), 2003.

Ajzen, I. The theory of planned behavior. *Organizational Behavior and Human Decision Processes, 50,* Elsevier Inc, 1991.

Bhagavadgita. New York City, New York: Dover Publications Inc, 1993.

Boehm, Julia K. and Lyubormirsky, Sonja. *Oxford Handbook of Positive Psychology.* New York City, New York: Oxford University Press, Inc, 2009.

Carey, Kenneth X. *Vision: A Personal Call to Create a New World.* New York: Harper Collins Publications, 1985.

Conference centres on adolescent brain development (online, http://mywebtimes.com/archives/ottawa/display.php?id=366995, 2008).

Corby, David. *Vibrational Healing Systems, Brain Function 1, VHS Course 3.* Hornsby, Sydney: Perfectly Balanced Pty Ltd, 2003.

Covey, Stephen R. *The Seven Habits of Highly Effective People.* New York City, New York: Simon and Schuster, 1989.

Foundation for Inner Peace. *A Course in Miracles.* New York: Viking Penguin Inc, 1975.

Gottman's Marriage Tips 101 (online, http://www.gottman.com, 2004).

Hawkings, D. R., M.D., Ph.D. *Power Vs Force.* West Sedona, Arizona: Veritas Publishing, www.veritaspub.com.

Krebs, Dr Charles. *Foundations of Holistic Kinesiology.* Applied Physiology, 2001.

Yogananda, Paramahansa. *The Law of Success.* Los Angeles, California: Self-Realization Fellowship, 1944.

recommended reading

Foundation for Inner Peace. *A Course in Miracles.* New York, New York: Viking Penguin Inc, 1975.

Bradden, Gregg. *The Divine Matrix.* Carlsbad, California: Hay House Inc, 2008.

Cornelius, Helena and Faire, Shoshana. *Everyone Can Win.* Sydney, New South Wales: Simon and Schuster Australia, 1989.

Corkhill Briggs, Dorothy. *Your Child's Self-Esteem.* New York, New York: Doubleday, 1970.

Covey, Stephen R. *The 7 Habits of Highly Effective People.* Melbourne, Victoria: Information Australia, 1990.

Donald Walsch, Neale. *Conversations with God.* Sydney, Australia: Hodder Headline Australia Pty Limited, 1996.

Hay, Louise L. *You Can Heal Your Life.* Sydney, New South Wales: Specialist Publications, 1984.

Hicks, Esther and Jerry. *Ask and it is Given.* Carlsbad, California: Hay House, 2004.

Legge, James. *Tao Te Ching.* New York, New York: Vintage Books, 1972.

Lipton, Bruce H. *The Biology of Belief.* Hay House Inc.: www.hayhouse.com, 2005.

Noontil, Annette. *The Body is the Barometer of the Soul.* Nunawading, Victoria: Annette Noontil, 1994.

Renard, Gary R. *The Disappearance of the Universe.* California: Hay House Inc, 2002.

Segal, Inna. *The Secret Language of Your Body*. Glen Waverley, Victoria: Blue Angel Gallery, 2007.

Yogananda, Paramahansa. *Autobiography of a Yogi*. Los Angeles, California: Self-Realisation Fellowship, 1946.

Even the least among you can do all that I have done, and greater things.

~ Jesus ~